directions

new

FOR
STUDENT
SERVICES

number 4 • 1978

new directions for student services

a quarterly sourcebook
Ursula Delworth and Gary R. Hanson, Editors-in-Chief

number 4, 1978

applying new developmental findings

lee knefelkamp
carole widick
clyde a. parker
guest editors

Jossey-Bass Inc., Publishers
San Francisco • Washington • London

APPLYING NEW DEVELOPMENTAL FINDINGS
New Directions for Student Services
Number 4, 1978
   Lee Knefelkamp, Carole Widick, Clyde A. Parker, Guest Editors

New Directions for Student Services is published quarterly
by Jossey-Bass, Inc., Publishers. Subscriptions are available
at the regular rate for institutions, libraries, and agencies
of $25 for one year. Individuals may subscribe at the special
professional rate of $15 for one year. Application to mail at
second-class postage rates is pending at San Francisco, California,
and at additional mailing offices.

Correspondence:
Subscriptions, single-issue orders, change of address notices,
undelivered copies, and other correspondence should be sent to
New Directions Subscriptions, Jossey-Bass, Inc., Publishers,
433 California Street, San Francisco, California 94104.
Editorial correspondence should be sent to the Editors-in-Chief,
Ursula Delworth, University Counseling Service, Iowa
Memorial Union, University of Iowa, Iowa City, Iowa 52242
or Gary R. Hanson, Office of the Dean of Students,
Student Services Building, Room 101, University of Texas
at Austin, Austin, Texas 78712.

Library of Congress Catalogue Card Number LC 78-56393

Cover design by Willi Baum
Manufactured in the United States of America

contents

vi

editors' notes:
why bother with theory?

Student services professionals are practical people and rightly so. They have important work to do and pride themselves on getting it done, which leaves them little time for theorizing. Pressures to get the job done are constant—from the administration, from the students, and from their own departments. They are service personnel because they value helping others and the rewards it brings.

This posture has had its costs. Often they have to proceed with scarcely a blueprint for a very complex job. Ed Williamsen at the University of Minnesota often spoke of the profession as one of "ad hoc-ism," referring to the lack of theoretical guidelines. In a more pointed fashion, Cowley (1964), one of the pioneers in student services, noted that student services professionals are currently struggling with the same problems that afflicted them twenty-five years ago, and that the confused and irritating situation of the past has continued to prevail.

One of the reasons that progress has been slow is that there has been very little systematic research with a theoretical basis on which professional practice could be constructed. Wrenn (1959, p. 46), writing in the NSSE Yearbook, commented: "There is unmistakably a set of generally accepted value oriented aims or scientifically based understandings of human nature. In short, student personnel work has phil-osophic and psychological foundations which have only haltingly developed and are disturbingly incomplete."

In the past two decades important changes have occurred in the field. The 1960s spawned a great deal of activity in higher education throughout the world. Cowley's comments were made in the spring just prior to the Free Speech Movement that erupted on the Berkeley campus of the University of California in the fall of 1964. Following those initial disruptions, higher education was plagued by worldwide student protests, demonstrations, and violence. "Innovation" and "change" were magic words; at various times the process was initiated by faculty, by students, by administrators, and by many others involved in higher education. Student services staff increasingly recognized that old models of bureaucratic structure and *in loco parentis* policies and procedures were not capable of coping with the rapidly changing nature of the student body. In many ways the 1970s have been a reversal of the 1960s. A declining student body, a backlash reaction to the "outlandish" protests of the last decade, concern with declining test scores coupled with rising grade point averages, and fear of a job market unable to absorb all college graduates have created a conservative climate.

Is it possible to find some constancy amid such change? From its inception the college student personnel field adopted a developmental orientation emphasizing the importance of responding to the whole person, attending to individual differences, and working with the student at his or her developmental level (see Paterson, 1928).

This has been the philosophic foundation "only haltingly developed" referred to by Wrenn. While adhering to such a philosophy, student service professionals have had difficulty implementing it because their theories were also "only haltingly developed." One of the continuing aspects of the 1960s has been the extensive study of college students as *students*. This was foreshadowed by Harper (1905, p. 320).

> In order that the student may receive the assistance so essential to his highest success, another step in the onward evolution will take place. This step will be the scientific study of the student himself. . . . In the time that is coming provision must be made, either by the regular instructors or by those appointed especially for the purpose, to study in detail the man or woman to whom instruction is offered.
>
> This feature of twentieth century education will come to be regarded as of greatest importance, and fifty years hence, will prevail as widely as it is now lacking.

Beginning with the publication of Jacob's (1957) telling review of the impact of the college experience on students' values and Nevitt Sanford's (1962) compendium, *The American College,* research into the experience of higher education has grown at a surprising rate. Harper's prediction has become a reality. But it has not come about easily or systematically. In spite of the large numbers of studies reviewed and reported by Feldman and Newcomb (1969) just twelve years after Jacob, Keniston (1971, p. 3) was able to say, "We have no psychology apart from the work of Erik Erikson to adequately understand the feelings and behavior of today's American youth." Keniston's comment pointed out the critical gap in our knowledge base: We had no theoretical models which could effectively describe college students and provide us with a coherent picture of individual development nor a theory upon which we could base our practice and which might provide constancy amid the changing conditions to which higher education is subjected.

In the decade since Keniston's essay, we have seen theories and models of college student experience flourish. Most of these can be considered theories of development since they are concerned with systematic change over time while in college. In a relatively brief period, the works of the following theorists were published or in some cases, reissued: Arthur Chickering (1969), Douglas Heath (1968), Roy Heath (1964, 1973), Peter Madison (1969), David Hunt (1966, 1970), Lawrence Kohlberg (1969, 1972, 1975). These theorists acknowledge their debt to the earlier writings of Joseph Katz (1962), Jean Piaget (1964), Nevitt Sanford (1962, 1966), R. W. White (1975), as well as the early work of Erikson (1963). At the same time, the writings of person-environment interaction theorists (Clark and Trow, 1966; Holland, 1966; Pace, 1967; Stern, 1970) attracted interest and were beginning to be used with increasing frequency. Most recently, attention has focused on the adult years; Daniel Levinson (1978), Roger Gould (1972), Bernice Neugarten (1964, 1976), and George Vaillant (1977) among others have presented models of adult development which are important sources for understanding the increasing number of adult learners attending colleges.

Clearly, we no longer lack models of college student development. We have models, many of which represent careful data-based effort. What we also have are several new problems: (1) how to keep up with the knowledge explosion; (2) how to make sense of the many models; and (3) after understanding them, how to translate them into useful and helpful tools in our work as student personnel professionals.

This volume mainly focuses on problem 2: How does one make sense of the many different theories and models which exist? We believe that our framework will also assist in keeping up with the knowledge explosion and in making the transition from theory to practice. As a starting point, it is important to briefly consider the relationship between developmental theory and student services practice.

The theorist who has given us the most help in examining the relationship between student development and student services practice is Nevitt Sanford. Sanford has consistently argued that a college should be a developmental community in which the student encounters both challenges and supports. He has stated: "The institution which would lead an individual toward greater development must, then, present him with strong challenges, appraise accurately his ability to cope with challenges, and offer him support when they become overwhelming" (1966, p. 46).

From this point of view, development involves an upending which brings about new, more differentiated responses. However, if the challenge or disequilibrium is too great, the individual will retreat; if the supports are too protective, the individual will fail to develop. In essence, the student services field has to balance challenges and supports to encourage student development.

How does one go about such a task? What should be challenged and toward what ends? What actually *is* a challenge? Will it be the same for males and females? Traditional and older students? What is support? How does one, as an administrator of financial aids, create "challenge and support?" What happens in helping students put on campus programs that could serve as a developmental "challenge?" Is the task of having to cope with an "annoying, thoughtless" roommate a challenge in Sanford's terms—or is it merely a pain-in-the-neck which has little meaning in a student's growth? Sanford's challenge and support model delineates a crucial interface between the developing student and a personnel program. However, if educators are to encourage development, they must know what development is—what changes can, do, and should take place in students and what particular factors serve to challenge and support them. From our perspective, the creation of a developmental community requires a theoretical knowledge base which describes:

1. Who the college student is in developmental terms. We need to know what changes occur and what those changes look like.
2. How development occurs. We need to have a grasp of the psychological and social processes which cause development.
3. How the college environment can influence student development. We need to know what factors in the particular environment of a college/university can either encourage or inhibit growth.
4. Toward what ends development in college should be directed.

Knowledge in these four areas would give specific and concrete meaning to the task of encouraging student development. Such knowledge would allow us to establish feasible developmental goals; to design interventions that take into account "where students are"; and to draw on the processes underlying developmental change. Thus, given the purposes of our field, making student development theory work involves identifying how and to what extent a theory describes the nature of young adult/adult development and explains the process of developmental change in a higher education context.

student development theories: an overview

Originally, we turned to the theoretical literature hoping to find or create a definitive, comprehensive student development theory. We hoped this would lead us directly to the steps involved in creating a developmental community. As we searched the literature we found different theorists using different language to describe and explain different aspects of development. We were often left uncertain about the meaning of a given theory and even more often confused when we tried to compare and integrate the various models. We found ourselves asking: What does Chickering mean by the term "vectors?" Are they the same as Erikson's "stages?" Keniston's "sectors?" Are the "lines of development" set forth by Douglas Heath related to Chickering's "vectors" or Loevinger's "stages?" Are Erikson's "stages" similar to Kohlberg's "stages?" Perry's "positions?" Is "type" descriptive of people (R. Heath), the environment, or both (Holland)? The temptation to force the various models into one integrated theory was strong.

Perhaps the search for a grand design is always ill-fated; we did not find nor could we create, the comprehensive model of student development. However, our search led to a clearer view of the various theories, suggesting potential contributions to practice. The different theories can best be seen as a mosaic of necessary pieces. In fact, the theories seem to cluster into five categories or families. Each family of theories shares certain basic assumptions and similar constructs in describing development or pointing to influential factors in development. The five theory clusters are:

1. Psychosocial theories
2. Cognitive developmental theories
3. Maturity models
4. Typology models
5. Person-environment interaction models

We believe that each cluster provides a useful vantage point from which to view college students; moreover, these theory clusters outline the parameters that need to be addressed in a student development approach to practice. We will briefly outline the distinctive approaches of four of the families of theories and suggest how they may relate to each other. Because of their breadth, the person-environment interaction theorists have been described separately in another issue in this series.

Both psychosocial and cognitive developmental theorists provide us with ways to describe where the student is developmentally and explain how developmental changes occur.

Psychosocial theorists, building on the work of Erik Erikson, suggest that an individual develops through a sequence of stages which defines the life cycle. Each developmental phase or stage is created by the convergence of a particular growth phase and certain tasks usually viewed as learning certain attitudes, formation of particular facets of the self, and learning specific skills which must be mastered if one is to successfully manage that particular life phase. In general, psychosocial theorists suggest that development follows a chronological sequence, at certain times of life, particular facets of the personality will emerge as a central concern which must be addressed. However, the particular timing and ways in which the concerns are addressed is heavily influ enced by the society and culture in which the individual lives. Taking the psychosocial viewpoint, a student services worker would be interested in what age the college student is, what decisions, concerns, needs would be of primary concern, and what skills and/or attitudes would need to be developed in order to make decisions and cope with the various tasks. Some theorists identified with the psychosocial perspective are: Chickering, Erikson, Katz, Keniston, James Marcia, and Sanford.

Cognitive developmental theorists employ the structuralist view articulated by Jean Piaget (1964). Development is seen as a sequence of irreversible stages involving shifts in the process by which individuals perceive and reason about their world. The work of most cognitive developmental theorists has focused on identifying the *universal* pattern of stages that individuals go through and, in some cases, the typical ages associated with particular modes of thinking. The process of developmental change is seen as interactive: Individuals encounter problems, dilemmas, or ideas which cause cognitive conflict that demands that they accommodate or change their way of thinking to a more adequate form. The student services worker using this approach would attempt to ascertain how students think about particular issues and examine how the environment challenges and/or supports such thinking. Theorists included in the cognitive developmental group are: Harvey, Hunt (1970), Kohlberg (1969, 1972, 1975), Loevinger (1976), Perry (1970), and Piaget (1964).

These two developmental theory families provide complementary ways of describing college student development: One describes what students will be concerned about and what decisions will be primary; the other suggests how students will think about those issues and what shifts in reasoning will occur.

There are two other families of theories that add useful dimensions to the general developmental models. These theories raise special considerations not treated by the developmental models.

Psychosocial and cognitive developmental models focus on particular facets of the student, but student personnel workers deal with individual students who simultaneously think, value, relate, and wonder about themselves. Theorists who attempt to construct models of maturity, for example Douglas Heath, describe the often simultaneous changes involved in development. These writers try to synthesize the total developmental picture and may provide schema which subsume the specific, more narrowly focused developmental models. These models suggest long-range goals which student services workers may use to orient their programs.

The fourth group, called typology theories, convey the real

complexity of the developmental approach. Typology theorists suggest that there are persistent individual differences—such as cognitive style, temperament, or ethnic background—which interact with development. The typology theorists help us identify how different individuals may manage, delay, progress through, or retreat from developmental tasks. These models emphasize factors which create consistent modes of coping with change and collegiate demands. Generally, these theorists present psychological (temperament differences) or sociological (social-economic status, class membership differences) typologies which stress different patterns of socialization. Roy Heath (1964) is one typology theorist who emphasizes psychological dimensions. Individuals who have presented sociological models are Newcomb (1967), Clark and Trow (1966), and Cross (1971, 1976).

The typology theorists turn us from the universal to the particular, suggesting important differences which may interact with the developmental process. Emmerich (1968) has attempted to construct theoretical models of such interactions; readers particularly interested in pursuing that problem will find his analysis helpful. These four groups of theories combined with person-environment interaction theories convey some of the many complex factors that need to be acknowledged in creating a developmental community.

can theory help to guide practice?

We started with the premise that our field has been hampered because we lack a systematic theory to guide our actions. We have followed the course of research and theory development through the 1960s and the early part of the present decade. We are now faced with the more difficult question, "What is the relation between theories and the real life of the practitioner?" Some of our first attempts were to create classroom environments based on Perry's developmental scheme to promote intellectual development (Knefelkamp, 1974; Widick, 1975). While these attempts were moderately successful, we had to recognize limitations. More recent attempts to relate theory and practice (Parker, 1977, 1978) have forced us to consider the following.

The Is/Ought Fallacy. Theories of human behavior and the data which support them are *descriptive*. They are amoral. One cannot assume that a particular kind of change in college students, accounted for developmentally, *ought* to be fostered. For example, students often experience a move from dependence on parents to independence in decision making and value choices. Whether or not it is good to move from such dependence to independence is another problem. Similarly, one might observe that many students experience an identity crisis and infer that it would be good for all students to do so.

The culture, religious commitments, or some philosophically derived model of maturity might give a viewpoint from which one could make "ought" judgments.

Individual Differences and the Homogeneity Fallacy. Theories attempt to describe universal laws. To use a theory of development with groups of students (as one might want to do in setting up a desired classroom environment) suggests that the individuals are alike, at least in the important variables. Our experience shows that that is rarely the case. Natural groupings of students bring together highly diverse persons, often very different even in attitudes thought to be held in common. For a theory to be useful it must always be modified to meet the particular characteristics of the individuals involved.

Students and the "Human Projectile" Fallacy. The title of the Feldman and Newcomb (1969) book, *The Impact of College on Students,* best illustrates this difficulty. It is difficult to talk of the relation between theory and practice without thinking of such phrases as "applying theory," "using theory on students," "intervening in students' lives," as though students were an inert substance much like projectiles that can be twisted, turned, and thrust in directions that we referred to above which addresses the problem: Do we have the *right* to bring about our purposes? The "projectile" fallacy ignores the nature of students. We must recognize in our theory that students are alive, make choices, are as aware of us as we are of them, that they act as well as are acted upon. In fact, they are deciding, choosing, interacting persons whose nature changes as we work with them.

These problems have caused us to reconsider the oversimplified ways in which we first conceived of the relation of theory to practice. We now talk of being more aware of the multiple conditions in which we are called upon to work with students, and the many considerations we must make in deciding what to do in a particular situation. Theories have become sources of awareness to us, ways of organizing our thinking about students, suggestions of areas for exploration, and keys to insights about possible courses of action.

Lee Knefelkamp
Carole Widick
Clyde A. Parker
Guest Editors

references

Chickering, A. *Education and Identity.* San Francisco: Jossey-Bass, 1969.

Clark, B. R., and Trow, M. "The Organizational Context." In T. M. Newcomb and E. K. Wilson (Eds.), *College Peer Groups: Problems and Prospects for Research.* Chicago: Aldine, 1966.

Cowley, W. H. "Reflections of a Troublesome But Hopeful Rip Van Winkle." *Journal of College Student Personnel,* 1964, *6,* 66-73.

Cross, K. P. *Beyond the Open Door: New Students to Higher Education.* San Francisco: Jossey-Bass, 1971.

Cross, K. P. *Accent on Learning: Improving Instruction and Reshaping the Curriculum.* San Francisco: Jossey-Bass, 1976.

Emmerich, W. "Personality Development and Concepts of Structure." *Child Development,* 1968, *39* (4), 671-686.

Erikson, E. *Childhood and Society.* (2nd ed.) New York: W. W. Norton & Co., 1963.

Feldman, K., and Newcomb, T. M. *The Impact of College on Students.* San Francisco: Jossey-Bass, 1969.

Gould, R. "The Phases of Adult Life: A Study in Developmental Psychology." *American Journal of Psychiatry,* 1972, *129,* 521-531.

Harper, W. R. *The Trend in Higher Education.* Chicago: University of Chicago Press, 1905.

Heath, D. *Growing Up in College.* San Francisco: Jossey-Bass.

Heath, R. *The Reasonable Adventurer.* Pittsburgh: University of Pittsburgh Press, 1964.

Heath, R. "Form, Flow and Full Being—Response to White's Paper." *The Counseling Psychologist,* 1973, *4,* 56-63.

Holland, J. L. *The Psychology of Vocational Choice: A Theory of Personality Types and Model Environments.* Wathore, Mass.: Blaisdell, 1966.

Hunt, D. E. "A Conceptual Systems Change Model and Its Application to Education." In O. J. Harvey (Ed.), *Experience, Structure and Adaptability.* New York: Springer Publishing Co., 1966.

Hunt, D. E. "A Conceptual Level Matching Model for Coordinating Learner Characteristics with Educational Approach." *Interchange,* 1970, *1,* 68-72.

Jacob, P. E. *Changing Values in College.* New Haven: Edward W. Harper Foundation, 1957.

Katz, J., and Sanford, N. In N. Sanford (Ed.), *The American College,* New York: Wiley, 1962.

Keniston, K. *Youth and Dissent.* New York: Harcourt Brace Jovanovich, Inc., 1971.

Knefelkamp, L. "Developmental Instruction: Fostering Intellectual and Personal Growth in College Students." Unpublished doctoral dissertation, University of Minnesota, 1974.

Kohlberg, L. "Stage and Sequence: The Cognitive Developmental Approach to Socialization." In D. Goslin (Ed.), *Handbook of Socialization Theory and Research.* Chicago: Rand McNally, 1969.

Kohlberg, L. "A Cognitive Developmental Approach to Moral Education." *Humanist,* 1972, *6,* 13-16.

Kohlberg, L. "The Cognitive Developmental Approach to Moral Education." *Phi Delta Kappa,* 1975, *10,* 670-677.

Levinson, D., and others. *The Seasons of a Man's Life.* New York: Alfred A. Knopf, 1978.

Loevinger, J. *Ego Development: Conceptions and Theories.* San Francisco: Jossey-Bass, 1976.

Madison, P. *Personality Development During College.* New York: Addison-Wesley, 1969.

Marcia, J. "Development and Validation of Ego-Identity Status." *Journal of Personality and Social Psychology,* 1966, *35,* 551-558.

Neugarten, B. *Personality in Middle and Later Life.* New York: Atherton Press, 1964.

Neugarten, B. "Adaptation and the Life Cycle." *The Counseling Psychologist,* 1976, *6* (1), 16-20.

Newcomb, T. M., and others. *Persistence and Change.* New York: Wiley, 1967.

Pace, C. R. *Analysis of a National Sample of College Environments.* Washington, D.C.: U.S. Department of Health, Education, and Welfare, 1967.

Parker, C. A. "On Modeling Reality." *Journal of College Student Personnel,* 1977, *18,* 419–425.

Parker, C. A. *Encouraging the Development of College Students.* Minneapolis: University of Minnesota Press, 1978.

Paterson, H. F. "The Minnesota Student Personnel Program." *Educational Record,* Supplement No. 7, 1928, *9,* 3–40.

Perry, W., Jr. *Forms of Intellectual and Ethical Development in the College Years: A Scheme.* New York: Holt, Rinehart & Winston, 1970.

Piaget, J. "Cognitive Development in Children." In R. Ripple and V. Rockcastle (Eds.), *Piaget Rediscovered: A Report on Cognitive Studies in Curriculum Development.* Ithaca, N.Y.: Cornell University School of Education, 1964.

Sanford, N. *The American College.* New York: Wiley, 1962.

Sanford, N. *Self and Society.* New York: Atherton Press, 1966.

Stern, G. G. *People in Context.* New York: Wiley, 1970.

Vaillant, G. E. *Adaptation to Life.* Boston: Little Brown, 1977.

White, R. *Lives in Progress.* (3rd ed.) New York: Dryden Press, 1975.

Widick, C. C. "An Evaluation of Developmental Instruction in a University Setting." Unpublished doctoral dissertation, University of Minnesota, 1975.

Wrenn, C. G. "Philosophical and Psychological Bases of Personnel Services in Education." In N. B. Henry (Ed.), *Personnel Services in Education.* Chicago: University of Chicago Press, 1959.

*Erikson's theory of psychosocial development offers
a way of thinking against which we, as educators,
can measure who our students are and how the
college environment may inhibit or
enhance their development.*

Erik Erikson and psychosocial development

carole widick
clyde a. parker
lee knefelkamp

To understand Erik Erikson's work we must examine his purposes and
orientations. He found his initial professional identity in the Vienna
psychoanalytic circle surrounding Sigmund Freud. In his approach to
development he subscribes to many of the assumptions of the psychoanalytic viewpoint. However, Erikson has departed from, or at least
redefined, the psychoanalytic view of personality development in two
major ways.

In the first place, an understanding of individual development
requires consideration of the external environment as well as of the
internal dynamics. Erikson's is undoubtedly a psychosocial view; he
places the developing person in a social context, emphasizing the fact
that movement through life occurs in interaction with parents, family,
social institutions and a particular culture, all of which are bounded by
a particular historical period. In contrast to most other theorists, Erikson is an interdisciplinary thinker who draws upon diverse areas such as
biology, anthropology, and history in his attempt to explain the social
dimension of individual development.

A second departure from the psychoanalytic view occurs in the tone and thrust of Erikson's writing. Stated succinctly, he is a psychological humanist who looks toward the positive and adaptive capacity of individuals. He focuses on qualities such as competence, identity, love, and wisdom, and highlights factors which encourage their emergence in the individual's life. In his more speculative statements, Erikson uses an evolutionary perspective. He suggests that human strengths and the social institutions which encourage those strengths are both grounded in universal developmental stages.

Undoubtedly, his theoretical ideas are a seminal contribution to our understanding of the individual life cycle. The journey from birth to death passes through "seasons." Erikson's model of psychosocial development helps us to chart them; even more, it describes an underlying psychological principle which makes their sequence understandable.

the psychosocial model of development

Ego Epigenesis. When Erikson describes psychosocial development, he is essentially focusing on the emergence and development of the ego, a selective, integrating coherent agency "which bridges one's inner life and social roles (Erikson, 1964, p. 148). Erikson's description of the ego eludes easy definition; in general, it is that part of the personality—a rational-intuitive core—which brings order and clarity out of varied experiences. Probably the most recognizable part of the ego is conveyed by the term *identity,* the organized set of images, the sense of self, which express who and what we *really* are. For Erikson, the development of the ego and a sense of identity follows the epigenetic principle. Using the developing embryo as a model, he suggests: "Anything that grows has a ground plan . . . and out of this ground plan the parts arise, each part having its time of special ascendancy, until all parts have arisen to form a functioning whole" (Erikson, 1959, p. 52). Thus, Erikson postulates that the ego emerges part by part in a sequence which is dictated by a "master plan."

To clarify what Erikson means by an epigenetic principle we need to examine three domains: (1) a person's physical stage; (2) his encounter with society and the social roles he plays; and (3) his internal ordering of those experiences, his ego functioning. For Erikson, ego development emerges from the interaction of the person's internal growth with external societal demands. Physical growth and cognitive maturation follow a biological timetable. A two-year-old child is manifestly different from an eighteen-year-old young adult. Moreover, and most crucial to our understanding of the epigenetic idea, Erikson argues that we have evolved social institutions with roles and demands which parallel the different growth phases. Since each maturational phase occurs within a particular social and socializing context, the life cycle can be seen as a sequence of "biological-social" phases, or more properly *psycho*-social. For example, a two-year-old who is achieving greater muscle control, can walk, and has a rudimentary language, will be impelled by his inner drives to explore the world; simultaneously, his social environment (through his parents) will demand that he learn to master certain tasks and confine his exploration. This conjunction of abilities and demands requires mastery of certain tasks which contribute a part to his ego development. Obviously, the social roles and demands confronting a young adult will be substantially different; his ego development will center on those psychosocial issues which are ascendant at his place in the life cycle. The epigenetic principle simply suggests that the inherent pattern of human growth and its parallel social climate create a universal sequence of psychosocial phases. Erikson sees an ordered pattern in our lives because of these regularities in psychosocial experiences which dictate the form and sequence of personality development.

Psychosocial Stages, Crises, Polar Attitudes, and Virtues. Erikson has described eight stages in psychosocial development; as stated, each stage can be seen as a particular time in the life sequence when physical growth, cognitive maturation, and certain social demands converge to create a particular developmental task. For example, the typical six-year-old is acquiring increased muscle coordination and capacity to think about the concrete world; at the same time he enters school and must contend with demands for performance . . . can he hit a ball, learn to read, and play cooperatively with others? The convergence of his inner and outer world poses a basic question about his identity—can he produce? In much the same manner, each of Erikson's stages poses a particular dilemma with its own unique set of issues. In each stage, the individual will assume a "psychosocial" attitude which ultimately marks his evaluation of himself as a social being and contributes another facet to his identity.

Erikson defines the basic attitudes that emerge from each stage as polar orientations. In each stage the individual can achieve a sense of himself as a person who has positive personal and social capacities, or he may emerge with a sense of himself that is ultimately debilitating. Erikson discusses these polar orientations as "nuclear conflicts" during which an individual wavers between contradictory evaluations of himself. For example, our six-year-old probably shifts back and forth between feelings of mastery and inferiority. Obviously, the balance undergoes continual change; but eventually there will be a crisis point when a decision must be made. A crisis is not a time of panic or disruption: It is a decision point—that moment when one reaches an intersection and must turn one way or the other. Thus, as our hypothetical six-year-old moves through his elementary school years collecting experiences and reactions, there will come a time when he will have to define himself as a producer or non-producer. The crisis may be posed by so innocuous a task as speaking in a school program, or it may be created by a major problem such as being held back a year in school.

In *Insight and Responsibility* (1964) Erikson adds another "outcome" to the resolution of each stage. "Ego-strengths" have their roots in the developmental sequence. A relatively positive resolution of a stage carries with it a basic virtue, an acquired ego-strength to sustain life's jolts. When these virtues are carried into adulthood, they create a foundation which enables the adult generation to care for the young in all of the forms (making laws, teaching, parenting, creating new institutions) that such caring can take.

While an exhaustive examination of each of Erikson's stages exceeds our purpose, it is important to touch briefly on the childhood stages since they set the foundations for adolescent and adult development.

During Stage I (basic trust vs. mistrust), which spans the first year of life, the infant and caregiver relationship raises the issue of trust. At this point the child will have to "decide" if the world is basically a trustworthy place or not. In the next two stages (autonomy vs. shame and doubt, initiative vs. guilt) the child's growth impels him to explore his world first physically, then conceptually. His tasks center on learning that he can "master his own body" and that he can pursue his curiosity without fear of trampling on sacred territory. During the fourth stage (industry vs. inferiority) the child's maturing capacities in the context of the school environment require that he come to an evaluation of himself as a worker. According to Erikson, these childhood stages create images which the individual adds up to form a rudimentary identity. If these stages are positively resolved, one can see the child as a collector of basic building blocks, a self that is essentially trusting, basically autonomous, able to act and strive toward goals without excessive fear, and able to achieve capacities and attitudes which seem necessary prerequisites to establishing an identity.

Stage V: Adolescence (Young Adulthood). Erikson is noted for his attention to the process of identity resolution which becomes central in the adolescent years. Other theorists (Chickering, 1969; Keniston, 1971) have elaborated and refined Erikson's identity stage, extending it to the traditional college years. From our perspective, an understanding of the identity task is crucial to college practitioners; therefore our discussion will emphasize the tasks and themes central to this stage: the role of the environment in identity formation and the meaning of ego-identity. In addition to summarizing Erikson's thought, we will discuss Kenneth Keniston's work which helps us understand identity issues in the light of changing social-historical conditions.

Certainly our struggles to find or define an identity span the whole life cycle, yet Erikson notes that the task of establishing a workable self-definition is preeminent during the adolescent/young adult years. At this transitional life phase, the individual, beset with a changing body, is developing a mind capable of abstract, reflective thought which allows him to conceptualize ideas ranging from his life ten years ahead to the purpose of existence. He is simultaneously confronted by a society which is unwilling to continue nurturance without a return on its investment. At age eighteen, the individual can no longer just stay home without being considered a bit out of place. Through various agents from parents to college admissions counselors, society pressures the individual to make concrete decisions—particularly educational and vocational choices, which will in effect move him into adulthood. The epigenetic scheme suggests that the convergences of these particular internal changes and external demands create a central psychosocial task: The individual must ask and answer the questions, "Who am I?", "What will I be?"

In the psychological sense, the adolescent/young adult is a "marginal man." He is still the child of his parents; but he no longer looks or thinks like a child. He has impulses, skills, interests, and social experiences which are qualitatively different from those of his childhood and perhaps those of his parents. Yet he is not an adult; an adolescent exists in what Erikson calls a "natural period of uprootedness" (Erikson, 1964, p. 90); he must pause, reflect, and make sense of himself if he is to manage the complexities of adulthood effectively. The individual must take his childhood self-images, assess his present assets and liabilities, define his future hopes, and actively synthesize an identity, a core self-concept which provides a sense of sameness and continuity. If the person fails to undertake the identity task or is unable to find his way, he risks role confusion, a pervasive sense of alienation or diffusion in which he is unsure of the meaning in his life and drifts along on the path of least resistance.

Erikson's phrase "the identity crisis" has frequently been interpreted to mean a time of pervasive emotional turmoil or massive personality disorganization. While true in certain cases, this view is generally a misinterpretation: Erikson means to suggest a time of motivating uncertainty. The nature of an identity crisis comes into focus if we turn to the central identity question, "Who are you?" Typical eight-year-olds would simply answer by giving their name, sex, religion, family or the like. College freshmen often have moments of hesitation and give tentative answers such as "I'm not sure, well I'm so-and-so's son or daughter, maybe a pre-med, but I don't really know; I'm trying to find out." They look at themselves and see a complex collage of bits and pieces which do not quite fit together; they have to create some coherence in that collage.

In a sense, this life phase is dominated by the search for personal feedback and perfect solutions. Relationships become most important as a source of information and validation; as Erikson notes, individuals are "sometimes morbidly, often curiously, preoccupied with what they appear to be in the eyes of others as compared to what they feel they are" (Erikson, 1959, p. 89). Vocational direction is often a source of role confusion; young people search for the "right" career which will clarify their identity. Ideological issues take on importance, and the individual hopes to find a set of beliefs which will organize life and world. In many ways, the individual tries to collect ready-made frameworks which provide self-definition and direction; yet ultimately he realizes that his identity must be tailormade by his own creative, introspective efforts. Paralleling the search for "truth" is a certain egocentrism or narcissism. Erikson notes that these elements of the identity search derive from the shift into formal operational thought in addition to the "physiological revolution." We must recognize that a certain self-centeredness and the search for perfect answers are logical and necessary aspects of this life stage.

Erikson argues that coming to a sense of identity is most often tied to the making of vocational and ideological commitments. To participate in society, the young adult must establish a vocational direction and value orientation. These more concrete or visible aspects of identity both derive from and contribute to the "sense of identity" which Erikson emphasizes as the central outcome of this life stage. The issue of vocational choice often appears to be the focal point of the broader identity resolution task for men. Erikson is less clear about the nature of identity resolution for women. Douvan and Adelson (1966) suggest that it is substantially different. They argue that the issue of intimacy is intertwined or concurrent with self-definition and suggest women tend to establish identity around central relationships. Certainly with changing women's roles the issue of identity resolution may alter in form; in fact, the integration of vocational and family roles may be the focus of the identity task for some young women. Certainly this area needs further clarification as new roles for men and women emerge.

Factors Facilitative of Identity Resolution. One's identity is more than the sum of childhood identifications and involves the integration of a more complex and differentiated identity. The process seems to require (1) experiences which help the individual clarify his interests, skills, and attitudes, and (2) experiences which aid the individual in making commitments. The formation of identity is fostered by an environment which allows for (1) experimentation with varied roles; (2) the experiencing of choice; (3) meaningful achievement; (4) freedom from excessive anxiety; and (5) time for reflection and introspection. College can provide such a "psychological moratorium" which will allow the student to experiment and reflect in an environment that exists, at least in part, to foster such development.

The Meaning of Ego-Identity. In synthesizing the essence of Erikson's thought, a positive resolution of the identity stage results in a "sense of identity" which is experienced personally, validated interpersonally, and formed in the context of cultural norms. The person has a subjective core self-image which provides continuity and sameness; put simply, he knows who he is and can envision those qualities which are most central to his existence. With a subjective sense of self, the person can look back and recognize himself in the child he was ten years ago, or look forward and fairly accurately predict what he will be like in the future. Identity, however, is an interpersonal phenomenon as well. A positive sense of identity is reality-based in that others view the individual much as he views himself. Thus one's identity is manifest behaviorally and can be confirmed and validated by others. A positive sense of identity will be seen in a willingness to take on culturally-prescribed roles of adulthood and participation in the various rites of passage of the society such as personal or occupational commitments. The virtue which emerges from this phase is fidelity; a capacity to sustain loyalty to people and ideas in spite of contradictions.

The Social-Historical Context. We need to emphasize that it is the social context of the individual in interaction with his inner capacities which brings the identity issue to the foreground. The nature of a particular cultural-historical period influences the form or tone of the identity search. A stable agricultural society may mark the entrance to adulthood and specify available roles quite clearly. For example, for a woman growing up in the Kansas of the 1920s, the identity task was primarily a choice between two options: marriage or teaching. In contrast, the highly industrialized, fluid American society of the 1970s provides a broad panorama of possibilities: There are a multitude of available and acceptable life styles, and career options seem nearly unlimited.

Individuals who work with college students often comment on the changes from one generation to the next. Each generation of college students will reflect the broader societal milieu in the way it addresses the task of identity resolution. Kenneth Keniston (1971) has refined Erikson's identity stage by focusing on the psychosocial effect of a changing society.

Keniston is a primary interpreter of the psychosocial development of college students in the 1960s. He suggests that society underwent a substantial change; college attendance became the normative social experience for young adults, creating a "new stage" of development which he labeled "Youth." He suggests that college attendance is so distinct a social experience that it has created a new psychosocial task and the potential for additional growth.

This period of development is marked by a central psychosocial theme: the tension between self and society. During this stage, the identity task shifts from the individual's preoccupation with who he is to the dynamic tension between what he wants and what the society demands. For example, most college students must deal with externally-established requirements for getting into certain majors, certain graduate and professional schools, and so on. In so doing, they must contend with factors which shape them in directions they may not want to go. In various forms, the college years provide a testing ground for sorting through how one will reconcile individual needs and societal norms.

Keniston's research focuses on different ways that students managed the tension between self and society in the late 60s and early 70s, especially on the influence of the broader society in shaping the identity quest. The late 60s and early 70s were marked by societal turbulence; American society was compelled to examine the value-laden assumptions which marked its commitments. By concentrating on students who had taken either an alienated or an activist stance toward society, he illuminated the identity task as a reflection of its conflicts.

In a sense, he put a magnifying glass on the "final task" of Erikson's identity stage. His major contribution lies in his delineation of the changes in society and the impact those changes have on the tone of the identity stage. Since Keniston's primary research the pressure of the American society on college students has altered again, and it is likely that these changes are reflected in student approaches to identity. As many have commented, the student of the late 70s is vocationally-oriented and primarily concerned with access to a "place" in society. This fact does not mean that the psychosocial theme of the "tension between self and society" is no longer valid; it means that the "tension" is now being experienced differently. The altered set of social circumstances does not diminish Keniston's contribution; we still need to understand and acknowledge the influence of changing cultural norms.

Adult Stages. As the childhood stages seem to produce the basic building blocks of identity, the stage of identity resolution is a time of preparation and rehearsal during which the individual defines who he is (and who he will not be) and makes initial commitments that circumscribe his identity. However, identity is not fully established until adulthood. The adult years are marked by turning the sense of identity outward to engage the common demands of adult life, to choose someone with whom to live and love, to select and to work within a career, and to more clearly shape and live out one's values. Erikson divides adulthood into three stages, each of which has attendant tasks.

Young adulthood poses the task of creating a relationship characterized by mutual devotion and chosen, active love. The young adult must decide whether to fuse some parts of his identity with those of another to create shared commitments. Erikson expresses the psychosocial attitudes that derive from this experience as intimacy vs. isolation and their attendant virtue is love, the capacity for devotion which survives conflict and sustains the bonds between individuals.

The middle adult years are characterized by the conflict between the polar attitudes of generativity vs. stagnation. Erikson suggests that adult man needs to be needed, needs to teach; his task is to find a way to direct those needs outward to create a society which sustains its members. A generative orientation may be expressed in many forms: the rearing of children, the production of ideas, or civic participation. In essence, the generative person actively invests in the society of which he is a part. The alternative attitude, stagnation, springs from self-absorption: The adult turns his nurturant capacities inward, focusing on his own needs rather than caring for the welfare of others. The virtue of this stage is "care," an evolutionary strength that allows man to overcome his ambivalence and actively nurture that which has been created—children, places, ideas, institutions.

The final stage encompasses the years of old age. The individual is confronted with changes (always physical and often cognitive) which suggest diminishing powers. Simultaneously, society turns people from work roles to nebulous and often empty retirement roles. Erikson suggests that this phase poses the task of coming to terms with one's life—of attempting to affirm that one's own existence (and existence in general) is worthwhile, even in the face of death. If one's psychosocial history is positive, if social relationships are available, and if one's actions continue to have impact, then it is likely that the individual will develop a sense of integrity; if these conditions are not met, despair may follow. The virtue associated with a positive resolution of this stage is wisdom—the capacity to understand, to put things in perspective and to convey that understanding to the younger generations. Time does not permit an extended discussion of the factors in our society which may inhibit development of integrity; suffice it to say that our society has not developed adequate institutions or perspectives to sustain its older members.

Much as Keniston has focused on the college years as an identity stage, other theorists (Gould, 1972; Levinson, 1978; Neugarten, 1964, 1974; Vaillant and McArthur, 1972) have concerned themselves with psychosocial development in adulthood. These theoretical writings chart a sequence of developmental periods with their attendant tasks which reinterpret and add to Erikson's general map of the adult years.

As Erikson suggests, adulthood is marked by phases which add certain components to the individual's identity, such as, I am whom I love, I am what I contribute, and I am the values I have lived. Present theorists dealing with adulthood more specifically point out the focal self-concerns at different ages and link those concerns to changing role patterns created by normative sequences in family life, the structure of careers, and the aging process.

It is not our intention to summarize the work of these theorists, but rather to point to the existence of models which delineate the psychosocial pattern of adulthood. Hodgkinson (1974) has argued that knowledge of such phases is crucial to the design of administrative and staff development efforts. As this knowledge base becomes less tentative and more coherent, it will help us understand the needs of older students and provide developmental environments for staff members.

The Interrelatedness of the Life Stages. Erikson often stresses the cumulative and related nature of life stages. The resolution of each stage creates the foundation for the next crisis and defines the likelihood of coping with it. Continuing development may shed light on early experiences and allow the individual to reformulate and synthesize prior stage resolutions in a more positive way. Regressing to a prior stage is possible. Erikson points out that physical uprootedness or loss of psychological moorings can shake one's foundation and cause a return to such basic concerns as trust and autonomy. It is likely that entrance to college, while calculated to bring forth identity issues, also re-raises the earlier issues of trust, autonomy, initiative, and industry. At the same time as the college student is toying with the question "who am I?", he is probably wondering if his new world is a safe place where his needs can be met, if he really can do it on his own, and if, indeed, he is as able as his high school GPA would indicate. It is quite possible that an older, returning student in encountering an environment with new and different demands will also be pressed to reexamine the identity issue; in fact, it could be argued that the return to college is a reflection of societal changes which unsettle the self-definitions of adults, re-raising identity questions for further examination and new synthesis.

research

Erikson's work is highly descriptive and provides important insights into the pattern of personality development. However, he is a clinician rather than an experimental psychologist; his constructs do not lend themselves readily to empirical study and validation. For our purposes, a more specific understanding of the adult stages, environmental factors which affect mastery of those stages, and more objective descriptions of the "outcomes" of each stage are necessary.

Few researchers have undertaken the work involved in applying Erikson's concepts to empirical study. However, a line of research initiated by James Marcia (1966, 1976) serves as a major contribution both as an elaboration of the identity resolution process and as a prototype of needed empirical study.

Marcia postulates the existence of different ego-identity statuses which represent styles of coping with the identity task. From these criteria, Marcia derives four possible identity statuses: the *foreclosed student*, the *identity diffuse* student, the *moratorium* student, and the *achieved identity* student. They might be summarized as follows:

Foreclosed	Identity Diffuse	Moratorium	Achieved Identity
No Crisis	No Crisis/Past Crisis	Crisis Experienced	Crisis Experienced
Commitments	No Commitments	No Commitments	Commitments

Starting with a semistructured interview to identify college student status, Marcia and his colleagues attempted to define the particular characteristics of each identity status in a series of construct validation studies. Their work has involved 800 students over a ten year period. Generally, their findings suggest that the *moratorium* and *achieved identity* students are more "mature" in many aspects of their lives than the *foreclosed* and *diffuse* students.

In interpersonal relationships, *achieved identity* and *moratorium* students indicate a capacity for intimacy and a moral posture of awareness of the complexity of moral viewpoints, respect for individual rights, and reliance on universal principles of justice. In contrast, *foreclosed* students tend to be more involved in superficial or stereotyped relationships; they are also more likely to be conforming and legalistic in their approach to moral issues (Podd, Marcia, and Rubin, 1970; Orlofsky, Marcia, and Lesser, 1973). The active, conscious attempts to come to terms with one's identity seem related to a more complex, flexible, and autonomous orientation to others.

Individuals in different identity statuses seem to experience and respond to the college environment in rather different ways. In a preliminary report, Henry and Renaud (1972) suggested that moratorium students were able to effectively *use* the college experience in coming to terms with identity question, whereas foreclosed students remained "closed off" from self-exploration and limited their contact with challenging individuals or courses. Interestingly, one research study found foreclosed students to be the group most satisfied with their college experience (Waterman and Waterman, 1970). In terms of performance, however, achieved identity students attain significantly higher grade point averages than any other status group (Cross and Allen, 1970). Possibly the foreclosed students may come to college without the expectation or desire to undertake reexamination of their commitments. They may appear to invest little personal meaning in their studies. They demand little and may be satisfied with what the college offers; but their academic performance may be limited by their rather superficial orientation to learning. In contrast, the moratorium students actively involved in self-examination may find a wealth of stimuli in the college environment; for them, the college, in both its curricular and extracurricular domains, may continually open doors to greater complexity, making the task of self-definition more difficult. These students are aware of the possibilities *and* their own needs; they may demand more from the environment. With resolution of identity and identification of a vocational direction, the achieved identity student is likely to be less occupied by internal struggles and ready to turn his energy toward effective study; in essence, he is able to make the academic experience meaningful.

Thus students who enter college in various ego-identity statuses will be substantially different in their approach to themselves, other persons, and ideas. But ego-identity statuses are not stable personality traits; they appear to be a sequence of stopping points along the identity resolution path. Some research (Waterman, Geary, and Waterman, 1974) shows the freshman year to be characterized by change; many students who enter college with unexamined occupational commitments end their freshman year in moratorium status, unsure of a vocational identity and reappraising their goals. In fact, from freshman to senior year the most common progression involved movement from "lower" statuses to achieved identity.

It would be convenient to assume a developmental sequence: Starting with a foreclosed identity, students encounter challenge and complexity which throw them into a period of confusion (identity diffusion); as time passes and they become more self-assured, they begin an active search to clarify who they are and where they are going (moratorium); and finally, they are able to make those commitments which solidify their identity (achieved identity). Yet Marcia's research (1976) does not support such a clearcut picture. Some students stay foreclosed through college, others stay diffuse; some achieved identity individuals stay in that status while other inexplicably retreat into a foreclosed posture. These varied changes are probably a reflection of numerous factors, such as the individual's past history and the types of stimulus provided by the environment.

Marcia's work emphasizes description rather than explanation. We do not know the necessary and useful environmental factors which encourage movement from the foreclosed status or the shift from moratorium into achieved identity status. Despite these gaps, Marcia's work serves to make the identity task more concrete and understandable. For practitioners, the identity statuses provide a useful way of thinking about "where students are"; moreover, Marcia's assessment method seems amenable to small-scale action-oriented research which personnel practice must employ. Most important, these developmentally different ways of coping with the identity stage suggest that we need to adapt our programs to such differences if we are to take a developmental orientation.

implications

As is true of many developmental theories, Erikson's delineation of psychosocial growth does not include specific prescriptions for practice. His theory, however, is descriptively rich; it gives us a vivid and understandable picture of the individual's movement through life and of the sociocultural institutions which frame that movement. Erikson's theory offers us a way of thinking, a template against which we can measure who our students are and how the college environment may inhibit or enhance their development.

Using Erikson's perspective of the life cycle as a framework for encouraging student development, leads us to consider (1) the meaning of age-related stages; (2) the nature of an environment which enhances positive psychosocial development; and (3) the individual differences in coping with a particular life stage.

The Meaning of Age-Related Stages. In most college populations, the task of adolescence, young and middle adulthood will be in the forefront: resolution of identity, development of intimacy, and the establishment of a generative mentality. Given Keniston's discussion of the prolonged identity stage and the belief that older returning students will most often be in the throes of personal change, it is likely that the identity issue will be central for the vast majority of college students. James Marcia most cogently argued the central implication of Erikson's model, stating that "college curricula, procedures, in fact, a total environment should be set up to maximize the occurrence of the identity crisis (periods of actual search) and to provide support for their resolution. Identity formation will take place in college whether faculty or administration think it appropriate or not" (1976, p. 128).

It is important that a college encourage a readiness for the later adult stages. Don S. Browning in *Generative Man* (1973) suggests that a generative mentality is central to the strength of society and the health of subsequent generations. He argues that "modern man appears to be generative because he creates so much; in reality his problem is his nongenerative mentality which is seen in the fact that he cares so poorly for that which he creates" (p. 164). Adults in our society often seem absorbed in their own lives rather than invested in "giving back" to society. In a recent column, George F. Will (1978) listed some current best sellers, *Kicking the Fear Habit, How to be Your Own Best Friend,* and *The Strategy of Self Esteem,* suggesting a large market of readers who "watch their moods and feelings as they watch the bathroom scales." The current self-fulfillment mania gives testimony to Browning's point; many adults in our society appear stuck in the narcissism of young adulthood. A college environment, while encouraging the self-examination necessary for identity formation, ought to point out what "being mature" *means;* an adult turns outward to care for and sustain the society so as to enhance the growth of all generations.

The Facilitative Environment. For us, the five elements (experimentation with varied roles, the experiencing of choice, meaningful achievement, freedom from excessive anxiety, and time for reflection and introspection which Erikson suggests are needed to encourage identity resolution) provide a framework which a student personnel program can use to examine its functioning and define needed changes. If we take three of the five environmental elements and simply ask to what extent we make those experiences available to our students, we may begin to conceptualize the nature of an environment which supports identity resolution. How well does a student personnel program encourage experimentation with varied roles?

How well do academic programs encourage experimentation? Are courses designed and structured so that students actually experience being an historian, a psychologist, or an engineer? Is the college sufficiently flexible to allow all students the experience of teaching or tutoring? How well do academic advisors encourage experimentation with roles? Are work-study programs available and if so, to whom? If role experimentation were granted an important function, when would students select majors? How would graduate and professional school admission policies be designed?

How do financial aids programs function to encourage or block student experimentation? Is it possible for students to take "time-out" to work while on scholarship, to cut course loads in order to concentrate on a special project?

What roles are available in the college environment apart from the student role? How well does the residence hall program encourage role experimentation? Can students become designers of environments? Counselors? Administrators? Entrepreneurs, i.e., student-run bookstores, snack shops, other small businesses? How well do student activities, orientation functions, or volunteer programs allow students a full "real" participation? What roles are available for whom?

Do we structure our environments and offer programming opportunities which allow students to make real contributions? For example, are disciplinary boards constituted so that they actually attempt to deal with violence, residence hall damage and academic misconduct problems? Do fraternity/sorority advisors effectively work with student groups so that they can identify house financial and interpersonal problems and design problem-solving approaches? How effectively do student personnel staffs involve students as coparticipants in their attempts to study and resolve various campus issues, e.g., drug abuse, roommate conflict, or if meaningful achievement was a criterion, how would courses be designed and how would student performance be evaluated? How well does a student counseling staff encourage student reflection and introspection? How effectively are residence halls designed to encourage private, thoughtful interaction? How well are our programs designed to encourage reflection? For example, do programs actively involve students in thinking about themselves? When students participate in governance, is time spent in evaluation and feedback? In essence, do student personnel staffs spend as much time helping students make sense of their experiences as they do in designing those experiences?

We need to continually assess how a college can increase opportunities for students to actually try out roles that are "real," to produce in performance of those roles, and then to reflect upon the experience. The cycle is somewhat sequential; experimentation is followed by analysis/introspection leading to choices and commitments. Often our current practices reverse that sequence and we may run the risk of premature foreclosure in many areas of student lives.

Individual Differences. The guidelines above present an oversimplified view of a developmental environment. Marcia's presentation of ego-identity statuses suggest that those five conditions will be effective for students at certain identity statuses and not for others.

For moratorium students, college entrance may be a jolting experience, but one which they are competent to handle. They are sufficiently autonomous to actively use this environment for self-definition purposes. They will likely be drawn to a diversity of peer relationships; they will probably be able to perceive coursework as a means to try out different modes of thinking, to seek out the complexity of social realities. An environment which makes possible wide ranging experimentation, achievement and time for reflection should provide the basic conditions for identity resolution. Given the moratorium students' active search, a career advising program which points out vocational options and the means to explore them, or an orientation program which lays out available activities, will be "developmental." As these students compile a range of learning experiences, the task of integrating the aspects of self into a coherent whole is a major undertaking. "They need help in learning to critically assess and reassess their energy on to longer-lasting, more demanding tasks" (Henry and Renaud, 1972, p. 8). Programs which teach basic problem-solving or decision-making skills may be useful and important.

In contrast, the foreclosed student may need qualitatively different experiences in order to move toward a conscious self-definition. For this student, an identity crisis is necessary. The student counseling program will have to provide more than a smorgasboard of opportunities; it may need to offer a "special invitation" before this student can begin to undertake the self-exploration and experimentation necessary. As Henry and Renaud suggest, "These students need to be taught that their feelings, emotions and desires are valuable and valid, that the abstractions governing their lives are not ones they actively and consciously chose. And when (their stable world) starts to crumble, they need encouragement to actively enter into finding, experimenting with and critically thinking about new ways of being in the world" (1972, p. 8). For these students, programs need to be designed in ways which allow them to assess their needs, identify feelings, and encounter new and dissonant information both about themselves and the world with safety.

This abbreviated discussion should convey the importance of attending to differences in the way individuals tackle the psychosocial identity task. Knowledge of student status does not automatically lead to a particular approach; however, in career advising, residence hall programming, orientation programs, commuter services, and fraternity/sorority advising, these developmental differences need to be addressed in setting goals or designing programs if we are to take a developmental approach to practice.

references

Browning, D. S. *Generative Man*. New York: Dell Publishing Co., 1973.

Chickering, A. W. *Education and Identity*. San Francisco: Jossey-Bass, 1969.

Cross, H., and Allen, J. "Ego-Identity Status, Adjustment and Academic Achievement." *Journal of Consulting and Clinical Psychology*, 1970, *34* (2), 288.

Douvan, E., and Adelson, J. *The Adolescent Experience*. New York: John Wiley, 1966.

Erikson, E. H. "Identity and the Life Cycle." *Psychological Issues Monograph*. Vol. I (1). New York: International Universities Press, 1959.

Erikson, E. H. *Childhood and Society* (2nd ed.) New York: W. W. Norton and Co., 1963.

Erikson, E. H. *Insight and Responsibility*. New York: W. W. Norton and Co., 1964.

Erikson, E. H. *Identity: Youth and Crisis.* New York: W. W. Norton and Co., 1968.

Gould, R. "The Phases of Adult Life: A Study in Developmental Psychology." *American Journal of Psychiatry,* 1972, *129*, 521-531.

Henry, M., and Renaud, H. "Examined and Unexamined Lives." *The Research Reporter,* 1972, *7* (1), 5-8.

Hodgkinson, H. "Adult Development: Implications for Faculty and Administrators." *Educational Record,* 1974, *55* (4), 263-274.

Keniston, K. *Youth and Dissent.* New York: Harcourt Brace Jovanovich, Inc., 1971.

Levinson, D., and others. *The Seasons of a Man's Life.* New York: Alfred A. Knopf, 1978.

Marcia, J. "Development and Validation of Ego-Identity Status." *Journal of Personality and Social Psychology,* 1966, *3*, 551-559.

Marcia, J. "Studies in Ego-Identity." Unpublished manuscript. Simon Frazier University, 1976.

Neugarten, B., and Datan, N. "The Middle Years." In S. Arieti (Ed.), *American Handbook of Psychiatry.* New York: Basic Books, 1974.

Neugarten, B., and others. *Personality in Middle and Late Life.* New York: Alberta Press, 1964.

Orlofsky, J. L., Marcia, J., and Lesser, I. "Ego-Identity Status and the Intimacy vs. Isolation Crisis of Young Adulthood." *Journal of Personality and Social Psychology,* 1973, *27* (2), 211-219.

Podd, M., Marcia, J., and Rubin, B. "The Effects of Ego-Identity and Partner Perception on a Prisoner's Dilemma Game." *Journal of Social Psychology,* 1970, *82*, 117-126.

Vaillant, G. E., and McArthur, C. C. "Natural History of the Male Psychological Health, I. The Adult Life Cycle from 18-50." *Seminars in Psychiatry,* 1972, *4* (4), 415-427.

Waterman, A., and Waterman, C. "The Relationship Between Ego-Identity Status and Satisfaction with College." *Journal of Educational Research,* 1970, *64* (4), 165-168.

Waterman, A., Geary, P., and Waterman, C. "A Longitudinal Study of Changes in Ego-Identity Status from Freshman to Senior Year in College." *Developmental Psychology,* 1974, *10*, 387-392.

Will, G. F. "Spiritual Fads Alter Bookshelf." *St. Cloud Times,* St. Cloud, Minnesota, July 15, 1978.

Carole Widick is assistant professor of psychology at St. John's University, Collegeville, Minnesota. Her work has focused on the use of developmental theory in the design of counseling and instructional programs.

Clyde A. Parker is a counseling psychologist who is chairman of the Department of Social, Psychological and Philosophical Foundations in the College of Education at the University of Minnesota.

Lee Knefelkamp is an assistant professor in the department of Counseling and Personnel Services Faculty Associate for Research and Student Development, Division of Student Affairs, at the University of Maryland.

Chickering is that rare entity, a scholar-practitioner,
who stands between and bridges theoretical
knowledge and the realities of practice.

Arthur Chickering's vectors of development

carole widick
clyde a. parker
l. lee knefelkamp

In *Education and Identity,* Arthur Chickering (1969) presents a model of college student development and outlines sources of impact in the college environment. This work has become a classic for student personnel practitioners. In part, its wide audience can be explained by the fact that it filled a gap; few other models of young adult development were widely disseminated until recent years. However, its popularity seems to derive primarily from Chickering's orientation to the subject matter. His descriptions of students and college environments are theoretical yet recognizable and realistic; his thinking connects in a very direct way with the experiences of college practitioners.

In recent years, Chickering has addressed a variety of educational issues: the development of commuter students (Chickering and Kuper, 1971), problems of academic advising (Chickering, 1973), and in particular, the nature of educational innovation (Chickering, 1976). Although our discussion will give some attention to later work, our primary emphasis will be upon the developmental model presented in *Education and Identity.*

In the preface to *Education and Identity,* Chickering presents the philosophical stance underlying his conceptual work as an attempt to restore to higher education the alternative of focusing on the developmental concerns of students as these are relevant to the current social situation. This alternative stands in opposition to an education which has become technical and materialistic. Thus, Chickering joins Nevitt Sanford (1964) and many others who envision colleges as developmental communities. Certainly Chickering's position is very compatible with the aims of the student personnel field.

Before describing Chickering's developmental model, it is important to examine his objectives. In writing *Education and Identity,* he was trying to build a conceptual model that could span a continuum from the student as developing being to educational practice. He was interested in increasing the working knowledge necessary for good decision making rather than refining the theory and research base of student development. His approach to increasing working knowledge involved constructing a framework of the developmental changes occurring in young adulthood in a more detailed way than the foundational psychosocial theorists such as Erikson, and presenting it in a form which draws on and gives coherence to the wealth of empirical data on college student change (e.g., Feldman and Newcomb, 1969). Chickering's model of student development, while psychologically sound, is not the work of a "pure" developmental psychologist; it is the work of an integrator and synthesist. He has logically combined existing theory and evidence extrapolating a pattern of developmental changes in such a way as to make the role of the college environment more apparent in those changes. Chickering is that rare entity, a scholar-practitioner who stands between and joins theory to practice. Although this bridging role is vitally important, it is not without liabilities. Developmental psychologists will find gaps in his delineation of student development; practitioners will want more specific guidance than Chickering's work provides. Given his purpose, however, his work reflects careful and systematic thought and stands as a major contribution to our understanding of student development.

a vector model of student development

Echoing Keniston (1971), Chickering sees the traditional-age college student as a person in a distinct psychosocial phase defined by the emergence of certain inner capabilities and needs which interact with the demands of a particular college environment. Erik Erikson's (1968) identity stage is an orienting point for Chickering. Chickering states, "At one level of generalization, all the developmental vectors could be classified under the general heading 'identity formation'"

(1969, p. 78). He has correctly pointed out that "identity is so abstract as to provide only a hazy guide for practice" (1969, p. x). Therefore, he postulates seven vectors or dimensions of development in the more general task of identity resolution.

The seven vectors along which development occurs in young adulthood are: developing competence, managing emotions, developing autonomy, establishing identity, freeing interpersonal relationships, developing purpose, and developing integrity. As Chickering describes the vectors, one gets the sense that each can be seen as a series of developmental tasks, a source of concern, and a set of outcomes. For example, in young adulthood the student encounters various societal demands which take the form of "tasks"; the college years are a time when certain "things" must be done; the student must learn to think, become independent, and start a career if he is to manage college and cope with adulthood. The vectors specify in psychological terms the nature and range of those tasks. It follows that the vectors also define what the central concerns of the student will be, the tasks which will confront and tend to be sources of worry and preoccupation. Finally, each vector delineates changes in self-awareness, attitudes, and/or skills which are manifestations of successful completion of that task or vector.

Chickering postulates that development along each vector involves cycles of differentiation and integration. In each of the seven areas the student continually apprehends more complexity, shifting, for example, from viewing himself simply as a good student to the more complex view that he is a person who is an effective memorizer, a mediocre writer, a skilled critic but a weak creator. These more differentiated perceptions and behaviors are subsequently integrated and organized so that a coherent picture of himself is established. Growth along the vectors is not a simple maturational unfolding but requires stimulation. Drawing on Sanford (1966), Chickering emphasizes the importance of challenge and response: The role of the environment provides the challenges or stimulation which encourages new responses and ultimately brings about developmental changes.

Chickering also emphasizes that students are developmentally diverse. Some students will be in beginning phases of dealing with competence and emotions awakening to external demands and inner feelings; others will be already "awakened" and focused upon the task of integrating and finding a way of managing those issues which express their unique personality. Moreover, students in different colleges will emphasize the growth of different vectors, and due to a variety of factors, different students may have trouble managing different vectors. Chickering's central observation that students will be in different places developmentally reminds us that colleges cannot address the student population as a homogeneous lot. A description of the seven developmental vectors follows:

Vector 1: Developing Competence. Development of competence is an area of primary growth in young adulthood. This vector includes three spheres: intellectual competence, physical and manual competence, and social competence. Increased skills in these spheres lead to a sense of confidence, an inner judgment that one is capable of handling and mastering a range of tasks.

The college environment is a testing ground in which students are asked to read critically, assess the validity of ideas, define and solve problems, engage effectively in a variety of role behaviors from friend, obedient student, and roommate to committee member, decision-maker, advisor, and job-holder. Although it takes many forms, most students appear to ponder the question "can I 'make it' here?"

Increased intellectual competence involves many elements, most notably knowledge acquisition and the gaining of critical thinking skills, particularly the capacity for analysis, synthesis, evaluation, and creation of ideas. Physical and manual competence is an issue as well. At this age, individuals learn to use their bodies more effectively to master previously unattainable skills. Interpersonal or social competence seems to involve the development of certain basic interactive or communication skills. Students become increasingly able to work effectively in groups and to manage a variety of social situations from talking in class to meeting strangers.

If students can develop the competencies that allow them to handle academic work and social situations, a basic sense of competence emerges. This self-judgment can propel the individual onward to risk new experiences; these subsequent venturings pay off in increased growth in other vectors.

Vector 2: Managing of Emotions. The psychosocial timetable raises the issue of emotions to primacy in young adulthood. Development in this realm involves increasing awareness of one's feelings and integration of feelings which allows flexible control and expression.

Prior to this stage, an individual's capacities do not readily allow detached self-observation and integration of feelings and purposes. Yet bodily maturation brings out a flood of impulses particularly involving sex and aggression. The student's ego has not yet gained flexible control over those impulses, often resulting in a shuttling from rigid near-repression of feelings to loose, immediate expression of the momentary impulse. This limited ability to manage emotions is reflected in the common problems of residence hall damage, roommate conflict, exploitive sexual encounters, various forms of chemical dependency, and excessive academic anxiety.

The task is to become aware of the range and variety of impulses pushing from within. The increasing differentiation of feelings leads to the awareness that feelings can be trusted to provide useful information and can be expressed. The second phase of development, integrating feelings with other aspects of the self and achieving flexible control, leads the student to find and try new modes of emotional expression, assess their consequences, and ultimately come to a point where he knows how he will handle different feelings and has defined what will be expressed to whom.

Vector 3: Developing Autonomy. The development of autonomy is a major psychosocial issue in young adulthood and includes three facets: establishing emotional autonomy, attaining instrumental autonomy, and ultimately, the recognition of one's interdependence.

The development of emotional autonomy involves a gradual decrease in the need for "continual and pressing needs for reassurances, affection, or approval" (Chickering, 1969, p. 12). College students, in an environment which permits self-regulation, begin to free themselves from parental dictates as a first step in this process. Yet independence from parents is an illusory autonomy; most students persistently seek guidelines and cues which dictate how to act or think in various situations. Students shift gradually from parents to peers as a source of guidance; later peers are supplanted by the more impersonal norms of one's future profession or some other equally remote reference group. Finally, one's own thoughts, perceptions, and values become the primary motivational influence in one's life.

One can see the interplay between competence, the ability to manage emotions, and emotional autonomy. Without awareness of and trust in one's abilities and feelings as valid sources of information, emotional autonomy is impossible. Conversely, the capacity to stand somewhat separately encourages wider experimentation, thus increasing one's areas of competence and emotional control.

The establishment of instrumental autonomy is the second developmental task in this vector and involves the ability to make plans for reaching goals and to be mobile in relation to one's desires. This dimension of growth is often described as the attainment of self-directedness and includes the ability to identify resources, get help from appropriate people, and use systematic problem-solving methods.

The final component of the autonomy vector is the recognition of interdependence. This follows only after an independent stance has been established. With the sense of being an agent responsible for his own life, the individual can acknowledge his connectedness to others. He recognizes that a militant independence incurs costs—a blocked career path or estrangement from family. The mature student has the capacity to find the middle ground between "being one's own person" and slavish conformity.

Some growth along the first three vectors is prerequisite for establishment of identity. If the individual progresses on the first three vectors, he will have acquired different perceptions and new skills and a sense that he can handle both external demands and internal demands without excessive reliance on others. The question that logically arises from these changes is: "OK, I've proved I can cope, now what do I really want to cope with, what is central to me?" Thus, the identity issue emerges.

Vector 4: Establishing Identity. This component of young adult development is simultaneously the most central and the most elusive. It is so interwoven with the other vectors that it is difficult to distinguish as a separate developmental realm. Yet Chickering sees the task of identity as a distinct developmental step. It involves increased ability to integrate the many facets of one's experience and negotiate a realistic, stable self-image. It occurs as an inner sense that there are core qualities which comprise one's being in the world. Thus, the change is perceptual and attitudinal.

Movement toward a clarified sense of identity involves coming to terms with one's physical and sexual self. These areas seem to be the ground on which individuals try to struggle and sift through the differences between what they appear to be and what they "really" are. Gaining the ability to identify and articulate one's own psychological profile requires trial runs which illuminate the consistencies which "are" one's identity.

Establishing a sense of identity appears to precede, in part, the first three vectors. Arriving at an accurate, realistic picture of self seems to encourage experimentation in the realms where decisions are required: relationships, purpose, and integrity.

Vector 5: Freeing Interpersonal Relationships. Young adulthood, at least in the college context, is a time when major changes can occur in the capacity for interpersonal relationships. Chickering postulates that development involves increased tolerance and acceptance of differences between individuals and increased capacity for mature and intimate relationships.

The student develops attitudes and skills marked by empathy. He gains capacities that allow him to perceive others, to listen and understand different views without the need to dominate or pass judgment. Later, skills and attitudes develop which permit mature and intimate relationships. These relationships are characterized by openness, autonomy, and trust. Development of intimate relationships rests, in part, on growth in autonomy and identity vectors. Individuals can then risk commitment without fear of entrapment or loss of self. Growth along this dimension is reflected in attitudinal and behavior changes; relationships are viewed as a joint venture, and interaction is more reciprocal and empathetic.

Vector 6: Developing Purpose. In young adulthood, a major developmental change occurs in the ability to articulate the direction and goals that define the future. The development of purpose involves assessment and clarification of interests, educational and career options, and life style preference. Ultimately, integration of those factors results in setting a coherent, if general, direction for one's life.

Certainly society in general, as well as the collegiate press, pushes the student to address the issue of purpose. Yet for Chickering, making a vocational choice is not synonymous with development of purpose. A choice made prior to extensive clarification of interests, options, and life style factors may create future stumbling blocks. Effective development of purpose reflects and is integrated with one's sense of identity.

Vector 7: Developing Integrity. Defining a set of values that guides one's actions is also a developmental task of central importance in young adulthood. Students take a series of steps in this area: the humanizing of values, the personalizing of values, and finally, the seeking of congruence between beliefs and behavior.

Along with many other theorists, Chickering sees humanizing of values as involving the student in shifting from a literal, doctrinaire set of beliefs to an awareness of the relativity of values. The student gains the capacity to look closely and objectively at situations and incorporate complexity into his value judgments. In personalizing of values, the student begins to erect a personal code that reflects his personal assessments and directions and that serves as a flexible guide to behavior. With the personalizing of values comes the third phase of this vector, increased awareness of the relationship between values held and behavior and increased ability to attain congruence between values and actions.

conditions for impact

Clearly Chickering takes an interactionist view; he argues that a college environment can connect with students in certain ways which encourage development along the vectors. He outlines the nature of this interaction at a general level, indicating six components of a college environment which may influence student development. For each component, he hypothesizes conditions most conducive to growth. Following are a listing of the six components and Chickering's hypotheses.

1. *Clarity and Consistency of Objectives.* "Impact increases as institutional objectives are clear and taken seriously, and as the diverse

elements of the college and its program are internally consistent in the service of its objectives" (p. 147).

2. *Size of Institution.* "As redundancy increases, development of competence, identity, integrity and the freeing of interpersonal relationships decreases" (p. 147).

3. *Curriculum, Teaching, and Evaluation.* A. "When few electives are offered, when books and print are the sole objects of study, when teaching is by lecture, when evaluation is frequent and competitive, ability to memorize is fostered. Sense of competence, freeing of interpersonal relationships and development of identity and purpose are not." B. "When choice and flexibility are offered, when direct experiences are called for, when teaching is by discussion, and when evaluation involves frequent communication concerning the substance of behavior and performance, the ability to analyze and synthesize is fostered, as are sense of competence, freeing of interpersonal relationships, and development of autonomy, identity and purpose" (p. 148).

4. *Residence Hall Arrangements.* "Residence hall arrangements either foster or inhibit development of competence, purpose, integrity, and freeing of interpersonal relationships depending upon the diversity of backgrounds and attitudes among the residents, the opportunities for significant interchanges, the existence of shared intellectual interests and the degree to which the unit becomes a meaningful culture for its members" (pp. 151–152).

5. *Faculty and Administration.* "When student-faculty interaction is frequent and friendly and when it occurs in diverse situations calling for varied roles, development of intellectual competence, sense of competency, autonomy and purpose are fostered" (p. 152).

6. *Friends, Groups, and Student Culture.* "The student culture either amplifies or attenuates the impact of curriculum, teaching, and evaluation, residence hall arrangements and student-faculty relationships" (p. 155).

It is not within the sphere of this summary to give a detailed discussion of each environmental arrangement as it influences vector development. For that information, the reader is referred to *Education and Identity.* Moreover, the majority of colleges are not liberal arts institutions and do not share their singular orientation or residential population. Chickering's hypotheses are to some extent context-bound and are less directly relevant in considering other types of institutions. Particularly in the student personnel area, we need to understand developmental processes that can guide small, step-by-step efforts in program design and policy formation. Chickering's hypotheses in the form presented are difficult to translate into day-to-day practice; however, underlying those hypotheses is a set of implicit assumptions that may be useful.

In listing these assumptions, we must return to an earlier discussion. Chickering argues that development follows a challenge/response pattern; development follows "when students pursue tasks through which changes occur" (1969, p. 144). He means that certain activities will by their very nature provide information, demand different behaviors, and provoke introspection—all elements which bring about developmental changes in attitudes and behavior. Chickering's hypotheses define the institutional arrangements which best create experiences which are growth-inducing. Chickering's work suggests five major experiences or tasks central to developmental change. These are tasks or situations which: (1) engage the student in making choices; (2) require interaction with diverse individuals and ideas; (3) involve students in direct and varied experiences; (4) involve the student in solving complex intellectual and social problems without demands for conformity to an authority's view; and (5) involve the student in receiving feedback and making objective self-assessments.

His attempt to specify institutional arrangements that encourage development requires that we look more closely at the experiences and the task demands of learning and living in a college environment.

a critique of the model

While Chickering's work is empirically grounded and comprehensive, the breadth of his theorizing is not accompanied by sufficient specificity or precision. In describing the vectors, Chickering lays out the types and patterns of change in a global fashion. His descriptions of the vectors sometimes articulate growth in terms of an inner sense, while at other times he speaks in behavioral terms. A better understanding of growth in each vector requires delineation of component attitudes, self-percepts, behaviors, and sequence of changes, After reading Chickering's discussion one still wonders: What *is* intellectual competence? What are the steps involved in achievement? Greater explication is needed for each of the seven areas.

The description of the process of development through differentiation and integration, challenge and response is extremely global. He does not address different motivational levels of students, but tends to suggest that they will develop if they encounter situations which demand new responses. He does not delineate particular processes of change for each vector. It seems likely that becoming autonomous may involve steps different from those involved in becoming intellectually competent. One is left with many functional questions. For example, why does increased tolerance develop? If encounters with diversity really do encourage development of tolerance, are there certain types of encounters occurring at certain times that are more helpful? An adequate explanation of developmental change along the vectors requires greater consideration of motivational elements, as well as cognitive and behavioral change processes for each domain.

For this reason, it may be useful and necessary to draw on other more specific knowledge bases relevant to each vector. It is important to note that Chickering's work in *Education and Identity* reflected the best available knowledge bases at that time. In subsequent writings (1976), he has refined and elaborated his discussion of developmental dimensions by drawing upon ego developmental theorists (Kohlberg, 1971; Loevinger, 1976), and the organizational framework of Chris Argyris (1974) among others. It would be helpful if he also included, for example, the intellectual development models of Piaget (1964) and Perry (1970), and work on cognitive problem-solving and information-processing. This might bring the vector of intellectual competence into clearer focus. In the area of purpose, material from career development theorists and researchers (Crites, 1974; Holland, 1966; Super, 1969) may augment his general outline. However, he continues to be a comprehensive and synthetic thinker. The strength of his work lies in his ability to convey the broad picture; the weaknesses stem from a lack of specificity.

research

Chickering's Research Approach. In part, the empirical foundation for *Education and Identity* is the Project on Student Development in Small Colleges, a cross-sectional and longitudinal study of thirteen liberal arts colleges undertaken in the 1960s. The purpose of the study was to identify the effects of interaction between student characteristics and collegiate press on attrition and personality change.

A major strength in his research approach is the use of multiple measures for assessing both college goals and student characteristics. Measurement of student characteristics and change was obtained through responses to a biographical questionnaire, an activity questionnaire, the Omnibus Personality Inventory (OPI), a religious orientation instrument, the Strong Vocational Interest Blank, and semi-behavioral ratings. Position and growth along each postulated vector was determined by drawing on scores or items of a particular OPI scale and relating those findings to other convergent measures. His presentation of the vector model directly incorporates his research findings. At times it is difficult to separate his more general hypotheses about student growth from his empirical findings. For the research-oriented, it would be valuable to delineate the specific empirical data on student change from freshman to senior year. However, for our purposes it seems fair to conclude that Chickering's empirical findings generally substantiate the patterns of growth hypothesized by the vector model.

It is important to note that Chickering's data indicates differential levels of development for students at different colleges. Some individuals appear to progress extensively along each vector; others make more limited progress. The extent of growth appears to depend on both student readiness and institutional press.

Chickering's approach to assessing vector development emphasizes face validity; for example, expert ratings were used to identify different OPI scales as relevant measures of a particular vector. This approach is logical; however, some assumptions of the vector model may not have been adequately tested by the instruments. In particular, Chickering's assertions about behavioral outcomes and the vector sequence required inferential interpretation of the obtained measures.

More recently, Chickering (1974) has studied the differential experience and development for residential and commuter students. In general, the results suggest that a residential environment more quickly and perhaps effectively promotes development, particularly in the social arena, e.g., freeing interpersonal relationships. For a more extended discussion of this work, the reader is referred to his *Commuting vs. Resident Students* (1974).

Convergent Validation of the Model. In the past fifteen years, many studies have been conducted that monitor change in student attitudes, goals, and behavior during college. Feldman and Newcomb (1969) review the empirical literature, and Astin (1977) reports on a nationwide study of 200,000 students. The cumulated data and basic conclusions which derive from these studies closely parallel the developmental outcomes that Chickering postulates, although the majority of this research has been designed from an atheoretical stance and therefore does not directly test some of the assumptions in Chickering's model.

For specific vectors, the pattern of changes Chickering outlines is generally supported and discussed in greater detail by other developmental research. Jane Loevinger's (1976) work in the area of ego development indicates a stage shift marked by an interpersonal orientation emphasizing empathy, reciprocity and tolerance, and differentiated inner feelings that normally occurs in young adulthood. Her findings closely mirror Chickering's descriptions of development in managing emotions and freeing interpersonal relationships. Perry (1970) found that college age students develop increasingly complex assumptions about knowledge that are manifest in an increased ability to perform intellectual and academic work; his findings correspond and add a dimension to the vector of intellectual competence. Similarly, Kohlberg's (1971) study of moral development shows that the shift from conventional to postconventional moral reasoning typically occurs in young adulthood if the individual encounters more complex moral thought and has opportunities for role-taking. Although the assumptions are more complex, this work generally supports Chickering's delineation of the humanizing of values. Numerous career development researchers (Bodden and Klein, 1972; Holland, 1966) have found consistency and stability in vocational choice and direction to correlate with a more differentiated or accurate assessment of one's personality; this offers some support to Chickering's ideas about the development of purpose. These research efforts are samples of existing data that support general vector changes noted by Chickering. Yet much of the research has a different, narrower focus and hence does not validate the comprehensive model. One does not find extensive support suggesting that Chickering's model is the best conceptualization of the pattern of developmental changes in young adulthood, nor is there extensive support for the presumed sequence in which students address the vectors.

Elaboration of the Vector Model. As previously stated, a major problem has been the difficulty of expressing Chickering's vectors in concrete behavior and attitudes. Prince, Miller, and Winston (1974) have tried to make Chickering's vector concepts more specific. The Student Development Task Inventory (SDTI) has been empirically derived to serve as an aid to practice.

Prince and associates have attempted to translate Chickering's vectors into behavioral statements. Their assumption is that a particular pattern of behavior will demonstrate mastery of a particular vector. Moreover, since development is sequential and cumulative, certain behaviors will precede and be required for the acquisition of other behaviors. Thus, the SDTI defines development in behavioral terms along three vectors: autonomy, interpersonal relationships, and purpose. As an instrument, the SDTI lends itself to socially desirable response sets; however, it is intended for use in an individualized quasi-counseling approach which makes that limitation less important.

implications

Chickering's model delineates the issues and tasks central to young adulthood, suggests general patterns of attitudinal/behavioral changes in the seven thematic areas, and provides hints about experiences which facilitate developmental outcomes. Like all theoretical models, Chickering's work gives us a way of looking at our students that may help us to understand them better and therefore may increase our ability to conceptualize developmentally-oriented student personnel work.

The seven vectors seem to represent central themes in the lives of traditional-age college students. Apart from specific attempts to encourage development, our programs may be more useful if we can provide information and opportunities for students to consider issues of competence, autonomy, and so on. Chickering's model can serve as an index to the range of programming needed, which might help us avoid devising programs based on fad or staff expertise.

A college campus is a microcosm of the broader society and the press of that society may serve to focus attention rather narrowly on certain developmental domains. Students in the 1960s and early 1970s concentrated on freeing interpersonal relations, identity, and integrity; student personnel efforts at that time emphasized sensitivity groups and social-political programming. In the late 70s concern seems to center on issues of competence and purpose; student personnel activity reflects this, with effort concentrating on academic preparedness and career advising. While student personnel programs may reflect expressed student needs, a mature and effective adulthood rests on some consideration of all developmental areas. Thus Chickering's model may alert us to areas where attention is needed. These areas might be overlooked if programs and policies are designed solely on the basis of societal press.

The vectors are supposed to have a sequential pattern; programs and policies may be most effective if we at least consider that sequence as a plausible developmental hypothesis. Mastery of the first three vectors prepares the individual for the identity vector, which in turn paves the way for attention to the last three vectors. Any programming effort requires assessment of students to identify their developmental status; however, it may be feasible to suggest that the freshman year is a time when attention centers on issues of competence, managing of emotions, and autonomy. The student is more likely to respond and develop when student personnel efforts fit his priority issues. For example, freshman programs in residence halls, orientation, and advising functions may best relate to student needs if they focus on academic/social competence concerns rather than issues of intimacy or vocational decision-making. It may be that efforts to engage students in the personalizing of values may best fit later college years, after the student has a clearer conception of himself.

The vector model can serve as a framework for examining services provided and analyzing problems peculiar to those services. For example, many financial aid programs are beset with students who default on payments or "blow their checks" in the first month of the semester. It is plausible to explain that problem as a lack of instrumental autonomy. This analysis would suggest a developmental function for financial aids programs, teaching students how to plan and budget finances. Such an educative emphasis would have dual payoffs: a decrease in administrative clean-ups and student development of a useful skill. Three similar analyses of problem areas are included below as samples of this use of Chickering's work.

Residence hall damage	lack of ability to manage emotions, lack of instrumental autonomy	workshops focus on anger/aggression; methods of communicating needs
Residence hall staff overoccupied by roommate conflict problems	lack of ability to manage emotions, lack of emotional independence	workshops on conflict management skills in residence hall floors
Ineffective student participation on governance committees	lack of social competence; lack of instrumental autonomy	efforts to teach skills in group dynamics, leadership, problem-solving

Chickering's explanation of the process of development does not clarify how a student personnel program can be structured to encourage growth. It is unlikely that student personnel staff can bring about change in such areas as the clarity and consistency of institutional objectives. However, we can use the five abstracted process elements, e.g., choice, diversity, direct experience, as aspects of structure in residence halls, student activities, academic advising, and intramural programs. Two efforts to encourage student development will be given as examples. They represent slightly different ways of using the vector model as a guiding framework on which specific methods are built.

Prince, Miller, and Winston have proposed a program to "systematically facilitate the development of autonomy, interpersonal relationships, and life purpose" (1974, p. 2). Their program draws on the behavioral learning domain assuming that the vectors are comprised of learnable attitudes and skills.

The process is individualized approximating a counseling relationship. Following assessment of development using the SDTI, the student in collaboration with the student personnel worker engages in a series of steps to develop needed and desired skills. Together, the student and mentor define relevant developmental goals, establish specific, behaviorally-defined objectives, develop action steps involving particular experiences which can allow or bring about the learning sought, implement the plan, and evaluate progress. The student personnel worker serves as a resource to aid the student in defining useful developmental experiences. The worker draws on his knowledge of growth, learning principles, and the nature of different experiences to logically extrapolate the nature and types of activity which would be most likely to lead to certain types of vector-related growth. A model like this was recently tested by Thoni (1977) and found to be workable.

Kirk Lamb, director of counseling services at St. John's University, has also taken the vectors as a point of orientation for designing programming efforts. Lamb (1978) uses the seven vectors in a developmental wheel which outlines the domain of student growth and professional activity. For each vector, he has drawn on various knowledge bases to delineate component coping or life skills that seem related to mastery of the tasks posed by that vector. For the establishment of intellectual competence, he suggests that skills in organizing, methods of study, class skills such as note-taking, time management, test-taking strategies, and approaches to paper-writing will be enabling. For social competence, coping skills include listening, leveling or effective giving of feedback, and self-assertion behaviors.

From this point, he uses a psychoeducational design process (Snelbecker, 1974) to identify approaches for the direct teaching of such skills. Drawing on various sources (principles of cognitive and behavioral change, instruction technologies, counseling strategies), he outlines and designs the content and processes of a specific program. In general his approach emphasizes a laboratory education model; specific programs in the different vector areas are offered as workshops through the counseling office, in residence halls, and as a component of academic courses, such as test-taking and time management workshops.

This discussion of implications has not described what one does in taking a developmental approach. Rather, it has tried to show how Chickering's vector model can be used to understand students. It has also attempted to clarify the idea that encouraging development requires that one draw upon other sources in the design of environments and programs to provide challenges to development.

references

Argyris, C. *The Applicability of Organizational Sociology*. Oxford, England: Cambridge University Press, 1974.

Astin, A. *Four Critical Years: Effects of College on Beliefs, Attitudes, and Knowledge*. San Francisco: Jossey-Bass, 1977.

Bodden, J. L., and Klein, A. J. "Cognitive Complexity and Appropriate Vocational Choice: Another Look." *Journal of Counseling Psychology*, 1972, *19* (3), 257–258.

Chickering, A. *Education and Identity*. San Francisco: Jossey-Bass, 1969.

Chickering, A. "Culture Sophistication and College Experience." *Educational Record,* 1971, *52,* 125-128.

Chickering, A. "College Advising for the 1970s." In J. Katz (Ed.), *New Directions for Higher Education: Services for Students,* no. 3. San Francisco: Jossey-Bass, 1973.

Chickering, A. *Commuting vs. Resident Students.* San Francisco: Jossey-Bass, 1974.

Chickering, A. "A Conceptual Framework for Educational Alternatives at Empire State College." ERIC Document, ED 127 857, April 1976.

Chickering, A., and Kuper, E. "Educational Outcomes for Commuters and Residents." *Educational Record,* 1971, *52,* 255-261.

Crites, J. O. "Career Development Process: A Model of Vocational Maturity." In E. Herr (Ed.), *Vocational Guidelines and Human Development.* Boston: Houghton Mifflin, 1974.

Erikson, E. H. *Identity: Youth and Crisis.* New York: W. W. Norton and Co., 1968.

Feldman, K., and Newcomb, T. R. *The Impact of College on Students.* San Francisco: Jossey-Bass, 1969.

Holland, J. L. *The Psychology of Vocational Choice: A Theory of Personality Types and Model Environments.* Wathore, Mass.: Blaisdell, 1966.

Keniston, K. *Youth and Dissent.* New York: Harcourt, Brace, Jovanovich, Inc., 1971.

Kohlberg, L. "The Concepts of Developmental Psychology as the Central Guide to Education: Example From Cognitive, Moral, and Psychological Education." In M. Reynolds (Ed.), *Psychology and the Process of Schooling in the Next Decade.* U.S. Office of Education, 1971.

Lamb, K. Personal communication, 1978.

Loevinger, J. *Ego Development: Conceptions and Theories.* San Francisco: Jossey-Bass, 1976.

Perry, W., Jr. *Forms of Intellectual and Ethical Development in the College Years: A Scheme.* New York: Holt, Rinehart, and Winston, 1970.

Piaget, J. *Judgment and Reasoning in the Child.* Patterson, N.J.: Littlefield Adams and Co., 1964.

Prince, J. S., Miller, T. K., and Winston, R. B. *Student Developmental Task Inventory Guidelines.* Athens, Ga.: Student Development Associates, 1974.

Sanford, N. "Freshman Personality: A Stage in Human Development." In N. Sanford (Ed.), *College and Character.* New York: John Wiley, 1964.

Sanford, N. *Self and Society.* New York: Atherton Press, 1966.

Snelbecker, G. *Learning Theory, Instructional Theory, and Psychoeducational Design.* New York: McGraw-Hill, 1974.

Super, D. E. "Vocational Development Theory." *The Counseling Psychologist,* 1969, *2,* 2-14.

Thoni, R. "Differential Effects of Selected Guidance Strategies on Developmental Change in College Freshmen." Doctoral dissertation, University of Minnesota, 1977.

*The ways in which people come to think about and
take responsibility for what they know, believe, and
value changes dramatically between adolescence and
adulthood. Perry's scheme of intellectual and ethical
development, grounded in cognitive development
theory, charts the process of this developmental sequence.*

William Perry's theory of intellectual and ethical development

patricia m. king

Jean Piaget: the foundation of developmental psychology

To understand the context for this chapter and the next, it is important to review very briefly the work of Jean Piaget, who is recognized
for his studies of intellectual development in children and adolescents.
Kohlberg (1971), among others, credits Piaget with creating the structure for a powerful developmental psychology. Piaget's primary contribution to college personnel practice derives from the form of his theorizing or meta-theory. For that reason his description of specific stages
of intellectual development will not be included; rather we will emphasize his discussion of the nature of development.

The three fundamental ideas of the cognitive developmental
approach (Rest, 1973) were first and most fully explicated by Piaget.
His pioneering work has served to lay the groundwork, establishing and
validating specific developmental principles and constructs which the
two following theories have employed. The three central cognitive
developmental assumptions are:

Structural Organization. Cognitive developmental theories take
what is commonly described as an "information processing view" of the

individual. A person is an active interpreter of the outside world, that is, an interpreter who selectively attends to stimuli, imposes a "meaningful" order onto the stimuli that are comprehended, who develops and uses principles and rules to guide behavior and solve problems. Bieri (1971) suggests that the individual's way of processing information is determined by "relatively fixed patterns for experiencing his world . . . patterns which we may refer to as cognitive structures" (p. 178). Other terms which have been used to describe these internal organizing structures are "schemes," "conceptual systems," "personal constructs," "forms," "styles," "plans," and "programs." Whatever the particular label, these models assume a mediating structure or filter to be the major element determining how the person will translate and interact with external reality. From this perspective, cognitive structure is to be inferred from behavior or, rather, patterns of behavior, particularly those which reflect thought processes.

Developmental Sequence. Development is seen as a progression along a hierarchical continuum which is divided into a sequence of stages, with each stage representing a qualitatively different way of thinking. Each stage represents a more differentiated and integrated structural organization subsuming that of the previous stages. While development is seen as sequential, it does not occur in a lockstep fashion from stage to stage, but develops unevenly over time. The goals of development are explicitly contained within these models: The highest stage is an operational definition of human effectiveness in that it spells out the "most adequate" mode of processing information or of interpreting stimuli.

Most of the theorists argue that development is irreversible. Changes which involve increased complexity in the cognitive structure cannot be undone. The meaning of irreversibility seems to be a psychological view of the idea that "you can't go home again." Once the cognitive structure is expanded to incorporate a wider range of experiences, "home" can only be seen by or through the new more differentiated structure.

Interactionism. Development is a product of the interaction between the person and his environment. Both maturity or readiness within the individual and certain elements in the environment are assumed necessary for growth to occur. In postulating the nature of the change process, the developmentalists appear related to cognitive consistency theorists such as Festinger. They emphasize the role of the environment in creating dissonance or disequilibrium; individuals are confronted by environmental stimuli which cannot be handled by existing constructs; this forces them to accommodate and alter their cognitive structure to admit more complexity. However, too much disequilibrium or challenge can become overwhelming, resulting in fixation at a stage rather than progression to the next stage (Maves, 1971).

Among Piaget's important other contributions to cognitive developmental theory are the following concepts:

1. Development proceeds at an irregular rate. Movement from one stage to the next higher stage involves two growth phases. The first is a readiness phase in which the individual is prepared—or, to put it another way, gathers the prerequisites—for a higher level of functioning. During this phase, it may appear that the person is at a standstill since there may be little behavioral indication of progress. The second or attainment phase is the more obvious; the individual becomes able to employ the set of behaviors characteristic of the next stage functioning.

2. Even with attainment of the next higher stage, the individual may be limited in his ability to apply his new capabilities in all situations. There exists a process of within-stage development, "horizontal decalage," in which the capacity of the person to use his highest stage operations is gradually expanded to include a wider range of "content" areas. In some cases, it appears that there is a particular order in which cognitive operations are applied to different realms. For example, Piaget has found that children employ certain concrete operations in considering the *mass* of an object before they can apply those same operations to its *weight*. Horizontal decalage is a concept which modifies the idea of development as a series of steps from stage to stage by incorporating the idea of gradual change.

3. An important contribution of Piagetian theory has been the identification of an attitude or "state of mind" that appears to accompany some phases of developmental progress. An egocentrism, an extreme self-consciousness, seems to arise when a person takes on a novel task, that is, the mode of thinking or "operations" of a new stage. Piaget has identified three major eruptions of egocentrism in the process of intellectual development. Two occur during childhood, while the other appears in adolescence as a by-product of the transition of formal operational or abstract thought. A major part of the developmental process includes "decentering", the shifting of focus from self to the larger world.

Perry's theory of intellectual and ethical development

William Perry (1970) and his associates at Harvard University developed a theory which outlines the intellectual and ethical development of college students. This nine-position scheme traces the evolution in students' thinking about the nature of knowledge, truth and values, and the meaning of life and responsibilities. The scheme describes the steps by which students move from a simplistic, categorical view of the world (described in such unqualified terms as we-they, right-wrong, and good-bad) to a realization of the contingent nature of knowledge, relative values, and the formation and affirmation of their own commitments. It addresses the interface between their intellect, the way they understand the world and the nature of knowledge ("How do I know what to believe?") and their identity, the way they find personal meaning for their role in that world ("How do I know who I am and can be?")

Perry's theory represents a continuum of development divided into a nine-position sequence. It is useful for discussion purposes, however, to cluster the nine positions by their common characteristics into four general categories.

Dualism (Positions 1–2). Students who view the world dualistically use discrete, concrete, and absolute categories to understand people, knowledge and values. Knowledge is viewed as existing absolutely. "Right answers" are the domain of established authorities and it is the role of the student to master these answers, or to learn simple truths. These students are likely to be heard asking, "Why do we have to learn these approaches? Why can't you just teach us the right one?" Tasks which require a consideration of options or multiple points of views are confusing, as the legitimacy of alternative perspectives is not yet acknowledged. Judgments or evaluations are stated as if they were self-evident, without being substantiated.

Multiplicity (Positions 3–4). Students who view the world multiplistically acknowledge that there are multiple perspectives to a given topic or problem, and those who hold different beliefs are no longer seen as being simply wrong. Questions which in dualism had single answers now have multiple answers. At this level, students are unable to adequately evaluate points of view, and question the legitimacy of doing so. They assert that points of view or opinions are equally valid, and are therefore not subject to evaluation. After all, they say, "anyone has a right to an opinion" and "you can't judge opinions." Students who reason in this way are often critical of teachers' evaluations of essays ("I'm being graded on my opinions") and are only beginning to separate the conclusion of an argument or opinion from its basis in fact. By position 4, students can see the difference between an unconsidered belief and a considered judgment.

Relativism (Positions 5–6). Students who reason relativistically recognize that knowledge is contextual and relative. Whereas in multiplicity the existence of different perspectives was simply acknowledged, in relativism these perspectives are seen as pieces which fit together into a larger whole; the context within which points of view exist has been established. At this level students show the capacity for detachment; they seek "the big picture," are able to think analytically, and can evaluate their own ideas as well as those of others. Authorities are no longer defied or resisted, but are valued for their expertise. This does not preclude their own judgments from being evaluated too, however. Relativists often resist decision-making. The merits of the alternative perspectives are so clear that it becomes nearly impossible to choose among them, fearing that to do so would sacrifice the appreciation for the other views. However, this often precludes or delays the establishment of one's own roles and responsibilities. By the time students reach position 6, they are beginning to realize the need to evolve and endorse their own choices from the multiple "truths" that exist in a relativistic world.

Commitment in Relativism (Positions 7–9). Students who arrive at the upper positions on the scheme have made an active affirmation of themselves and their responsibilities in a pluralistic world, establishing their identities in the process. Personal commitments in such areas as marriage, religion, or career are made out of a relativistic frame of reference. This allows for the recognition of diverse personal themes in their lives, themes which must be balanced pro and con much like alternative explanations are balanced in relativism. The process of "moving off the fence" of relativism enables students to better understand their roles in a pluralistic world by establishing their own identities and life styles in a way that is consistent with their own personal themes.

One of the unusual features of this theory, in contrast to other developmental schemes, is that it provides three alternatives to forward progression throughout the positions. These are "temporizing," where the student delays in a position, explicitly hesitating to take the next step; "escape," where the student is avoiding the responsibility of commitment, seeking refuge in relativism; and "retreat," where a student returns to a dualistic orientation, perhaps to find security and the strength to cope with a too-challenging environment. Thus development or forward progress through the milestone positions of the scheme's continuum cannot be taken for granted, as deflections to development may also occur.

critique of Perry's theory

Perry has described some of the fundamental changes that are posited to occur in young adults as they come to grips with the challenges of a college environment and restructure their own worlds in the process. He has accomplished this task without sacrificing either the complexity of human growth in general or of the collegiate experience in particular. His delineation of the social, moral, and intellectual development of young adults is comprehensive, and includes both the sorrow and exhilaration it entails. Its rich description of college student development is the strength of the scheme and the source of its appeal as a tool for understanding college students and promoting their development.

The theory is not without its drawbacks, however. In particular, it is very difficult to separate its underlying constructs, as noted by Boyd (1972), Broughton (1975), Heffernan (1971), and Kurfiss (1977). The focus of the first half of the scheme (positions 1–5) is on epistemological and intellectual development; the focus of the second half (positions 6–9) is on moral, ethical, and identity development. Consider the description and examples of the first five positions of the scheme: Students exemplify increasing cognitive complexity as they deal predominantly with academic issues, the nature of knowledge, students' responsibilities as learners, and the roles and responsibilities of professors. Consider now the last four positions of the scheme where the focus is on identity development and making a personally affirmatory commitment in a relativistic world. (For an extended discussion of commitment as a psychological construct, see King, 1976.) The relationship between intellectual and identity development is one which has long intrigued educators and psychologists. While finding both issues addressed in one theory has been a great source of its appeal (and has stimulated many thoughtful questions and activities both in research and practice), it has also made research difficult. Perry's description of the development of college students has attracted a number of researchers to investigate both the theory itself as well as its potential applicability. These studies will be considered next.

review of basic research on Perry's theory

Validating a developmental theory is a difficult and complex undertaking and requires a careful integration of results from a number of studies. The following investigations provide a preliminary empirical base from which to judge the validity of Perry's scheme. (A more comprehensive review of these studies may be found in King, 1977.)

Kurfiss (1977) investigated three characteristics of Perry's scheme: its sequential and hierarchical nature and the degree of stage unity within positions. A series of two-hour interviews were conducted individually with twenty-eight college students (fourteen freshmen and fourteen juniors) in which each subject was asked to respond to a series of forty statements. This series consisted of five sets of position-representative statements, each statement reflecting one of Perry's positions. Five content areas were included: moral values, counseling and advice, grading of essays, the responsibility of the professor in relationship to knowledge, and the nature of knowledge. Sequentiality was determined by testing comprehension of the statements, the hierarchy of the positions on the scheme was tested by reference to the subject's preference for the position statements, and stage unity was tested by factor-analyzing the comprehension scores across content areas and by analyzing the distribution of percentages of comprehension scores across positions. Levels of authoritarianism were also determined for about half of the subjects.

No significant differences were found in the comprehension or preference scores of the freshmen and the juniors, with each group preferring the Position 4 (Relativism Subordinate) statements most often. These scores were found to be curvilinearly related to authoritarianism.

Using a scalogram analysis of the comprehension scores, Kurfiss concluded that the position-representative statements reflected a sequence of increasingly complex and sophisticated concepts, as well as a strong scaling property. The evidence for the hierarchical property is mixed: Subjects' preference scores tended to cluster around their comprehension scores (within the range of -1 to $+1$), but this tendency did not exceed chance.

The factor analysis, used to test stage unity, yielded two primary factors: the first related to academic issues (the areas of grading, professors, and counseling), and the second related to degree of abstraction (encompassing the areas of morals and epistemology). The emergence of two factors here does not necessarily argue against a strong unified stage structure. Rather, as Kohlberg (1969) and Selman (1974) have suggested, the development of moral values (one of the two areas in the second factor) may follow development in other areas.

Meyer (1975, 1977) used the Perry scheme to investigate the religious development of Lutheran students enrolled in two small Minnesota colleges. He reasoned that there would be differences in intellectual development between students attending a private and church-affiliated college and those attending a public secular college, and that these differences would be reflected in the ways students conceptualized religious ideas. He hypothesized that the private college freshmen would be more dualistic than public college freshmen, that the private college seniors would be more committed than their public college counterparts, and that freshmen at both colleges would be at lower Perry positions than the seniors. In Meyer's sample, ten freshmen were matched with ten seniors in each college ($N = 40$). A structured interview format was used to assess the Perry position score, and in addition, each student completed the Harvey, Hunt, and Schroder

(1961) Incomplete Sentence Blank as a measure of conceptual complexity, the DIT (Rest and others, 1974) as a measure of moral judgment, and a Personal Belief Scale measuring conservative to liberal religious beliefs.

The average Perry position score for the freshmen students was 3.24, and for the seniors, 4.16, a difference which was statistically significant (p < .05). Contrary to Meyer's hypotheses, there were no significant differences in position scores by class across colleges. The correlations of Perry position with moral judgment and cognitive complexity were each moderate and positive (.45 and .40, respectively, p <.05) for each). The Perry-DIT correlation lends some support to Kurfiss' (1975) two-factor finding where one factor included the moral and philosophical aspects. Meyer's results are especially informative here, since this moderately low correlation occurred in spite of the religious content of his Perry interviews. This study demonstrates that students' understanding of religious issues can serve as a measure of their intellectual development, and that this type of development may be differentiated from both conceptual complexity and moral development.

Recognizing that all known research conducted on the Perry scheme to date had been conducted with students enrolled in liberal arts colleges, Blake (1976) questioned whether students in a science-oriented curriculum would show upward movement in Perry position scores over the college years. He used a sample of eighty students (twenty freshmen, sophomores, juniors, and seniors) enrolled in an agricultural college to investigate this question. A structured interview was used to determine Perry position scores for each of three statements adapted from Kurfiss (1975), relating to the students' educational experiences: the grading of essays, the responsibility of the professor in relationship to knowledge, and the nature of knowledge. He found a range in Perry position scores from position 2 to 5, with no students scoring at the Committed positions. The average position scores by class were: freshmen, 2.84; sophomores, 3.13; juniors, 3.55; and seniors, 3.48, showing a significant upward trend over the years.

Clinchy, Lief, and Young (1977) investigated the relations between type of schooling and the way high school girls reason about moral and epistemological issues, based on the theories of Kohlberg (1969) and Perry (1970). They tested sophomore and senior students at a progressive and a traditional high school, using the Kohlberg moral judgment interview (1973) and an epistemological interview designed by Clinchy and Zimmerman (1975) to assess Perry position scores. They found that seniors scored significantly higher than sophomores (p < .001) at the progressive school, but not at the traditional school. The two most frequently occurring scores for sophomores at both schools were 3 and 2. For seniors, the two most frequently occurring scores were 3 and 4 for the traditional school and 4 and 5 for the progressive school, suggesting that the educational environment of the progressive school was more conducive to epistemological development than was that of the traditional school.

King (1977), Kitchener (1977), and Kitchener and King (1978) have investigated the construct of Reflective Judgment, which focuses on how people reason and arrive at a point of view—how they consider the nature and role of evidence in their arguments, how they analyze and synthesize available evidence, and what role authorities and experts play in making judgment. This construct is based on Perry's scheme as well as on the work of Loevinger (1976), the conceptual theorists, Harvey, Hunt, and Schroder (1961), Broughton (1975), and others. The purpose of these two companion studies was to develop a measure of Reflective Judgment, and to investigate the relationship between this construct and two other measures of advanced intellectual development, Piagetian formal operations and verbal aptitude (Terman, 1973), among students at different educational levels. These studies used a cross-sectional design, with a matched sample consisting of twenty graduate students, twenty college juniors, and twenty high school students. A two-year longitudinal retest is now in progress.

A consistent upward progression of Reflective Judgment scores was found across the three groups, with the following mean scores for the high school, college and graduate students groups respectively: 2.77, 3.64, and 5.67. These differences were highly significant. Findings from these studies indicate that intellectual development continues and can be traced through the post-adolescent years and cannot be accounted for by either formal operational (hypothetico-deductive) reasoning skills or by verbal aptitude.

A limitation of the King and Kitchener studies addressed by Strange (1978) is that it confounds age and educational levels of the students in the three groups such that differences obtained between groups cannot be attributed to the subjects' age or educational levels alone. In an attempt to sort out this interaction, Strange tested two cohorts of students, thirty-two freshmen and seniors from a traditional age group (eighteen and twenty-two years old, respectively) and thirty-two "adult" freshmen and seniors (twenty-two and twenty-six years old, respectively). He found a significant class main effect, with seniors scoring higher on Reflective Judgment than freshmen; the adult students did not score at a significantly different level than the traditional age students. He also found significant sex difference, with males scoring higher than females. Chronological maturation alone, then, does not appear to account for differences in intellectual development that occur during the college years.

These three Reflective Judgment studies provide a strong initial indication that intellectual development does progress sequentially from adolescence to adulthood among those enrolled in educational programs. These findings are important for institutions of higher education, which are increasingly being challenged to demonstrate the effectiveness of their programs—not just in such quantitative terms as gaining more factual knowledge, but also in such qualitative terms as reasoning more coherently and persuasively. Knowledge of the levels and sequence of Reflective Judgment would provide a helpful tool to instructors in understanding students' cognitive orientations, and in promoting their intellectual development. The development of Reflective Judgment may be seen as an appropriate goal of higher education, for it maps the sequence by which "good reasoning" develops.

Another means of validating Perry's theory is examining its relationship with other measures which have theoretical relevance. Perry position scores have been found to correlate moderately and positively with those from Harvey, Hunt, and Schroder's (1961) conceptual level theory (Meyer, 1975, $r = .40$; Widick and others, 1975, $r = .51$) and with Kohlberg's (1969) theory of moral judgment (Clinchy and others, 1977, $r = .42$ for high school sophomores, $r = .70$ for high school seniors; Meyer, 1975, $r = .45$). These relationships are theoretically predictable: There is a common element of cognitive complexity germane to each of these theories, and growth on each is posited to occur in late adolescence and adulthood, but the underlying constructs are not identical; hence, the moderate positive relationship. One would not theoretically expect to find this relationship with other measures of intellectual development, however. Tests of scholastic aptitude (for instance, MSAT) have correlated with Perry position score very weakly (Widick, 1975, $r = .07$) and moderately with Reflective Judgment level (Kitchener, 1977, $r = .36$). Verbal aptitude (using Terman's Concept Mastery Test) was found to correlate highly ($r = .63$ and $.78$) with Reflective Judgment scores for high school and graduate students, respectively (Kitchener, 1977). No relationship was found between formal operational level and Reflective Judgment level (King, 1977, $r = .01$). These results suggest that developmental level is not a direct function of general academic ability nor of formal reasoning abilities, but that it is more strongly related to verbal aptitude.

application of the Perry scheme in practice

The Perry scheme has proved to be a highly useful tool for practitioners both in understanding students and in designing programs to promote their development. It is helpful in three major ways: establishing program goals, planning the steps in implementing the program, and in evaluating the effectiveness of the program. Two major applications of the scheme will be discussed here to exemplify how it has been useful in practice, one focusing on academic issues, and the second focusing on career issues.

The first major intervention program which was based on the Perry scheme was conducted at the University of Minnesota (Knefelkamp, 1974; Widick, 1975; Widick, Knefelkamp, and Parker, 1975). These authors reasoned that college students would respond differentially to varying instructional approaches as a function of their level of intellectual development, and secondly, that both academic achievement and personal growth could be facilitated by a proper matching of student development level with instructional approach.

Thirty-one students (predominantly freshmen) enrolled in a ten-week course entitled "Themes in Human Identity." The course had two sections, each using the same literary and psychological content base, but different instructional approaches. The first approach, used in the dualistic class, was designed for those students who had a primarily dualistic orientation, and served as an attempt to foster their movement toward relativism. The second approach, used in the relativistic class, was designed for students who had a primarily relativistic orientation, and served as an attempt to foster their movement to Commitment in Relativism.

Based on Sanford's (1966) conceptualization of challenges and supports necessary for development, differential supports and challenges were identified and used for the two classes. In the dualistic class, *challenges* were: (1) emphasis on relativism of viewpoint in the course content and instructional methods, and (2) experiential learning modes. Students were expected to gain *support* from (1) a high degree of structure in the instruction, and (2) a personal atmosphere in the classroom. In the relativistic class, by contrast, *challenges* were identified as: (1) occurrence of commitment amid relativistic, diverse content, (2) vicarious experiential learning, and (3) low degree of structure in instruction. *Supports* for these students were in this case defined as (1) existence of diversity in the content, and (2) the personal atmosphere of the classroom.

The most common Perry positions at the beginning of the course were positions 3 and 4; this shifted to positions 4 and 5 by the end of the intervention program. The range of ratings for this sample was quite narrow, encompassing only positions 2–5. Increase in Perry position score, an important indicator of the "success" of the intervention, was computed by comparing each student's pretest and posttest position ratings. Ninety percent of the students scored higher on the posttest than they had on the pretest.

The significance of this study lies in the identification of factors which influence developmental progress and in the use of these factors in the design of an instructional program. The choice of factors was theoretically justified and their use in an intervention setting was very effective.

This study stands as an ambitious early attempt to test the effectiveness of educational interventions based on Perry's theory. The issues raised by this study have been provocative and have stimulated a variety of new research endeavors, including a partial replication conducted by Stephenson and Hunt (1977). These authors retained the basic design of the "Themes in Human Identity" course, but used only a dualistic "treatment," and strengthened the research on this intervention by adding two comparison groups. Their results were consistent with those found in the original study, and greater upward movement was found for students in the experimental classes than for those in the comparison classes. These results offer additional evidence that progression along the scheme is differentially affected by the instructional approach used by the teacher.

These studies have demonstrated the importance of recognizing the design and structure of classes as an important variable related to students' intellectual development. Building on these findings, others have used the Perry scheme to improve programs in nonacademic areas as well. For example, Touchton, Wertheimer, Cornfeld, and Harrison (1977) conducted an intervention program in which the purpose was to increase the complexity with which students think about career issues. Their program used the Perry scheme as a general theoretical base, but because of their more specific focus on career development, they used the Knefelkamp-Slepitza (1976) Career Development Model, a nine-position description of career development based on Perry's scheme. Career development on the model is mapped by reference to growth in three areas (Knefelkamp, 1978): how career is viewed, one's view of career counseling, and career decision-making. Nine "areas of qualitative change" in which developmental growth occurs have been described: Locus of Control, Analysis, Synthesis, Semantic Structure, Self-Processing, Openness to Alternative Perspectives, Ability to Assume Responsibility, Ability to Take on New Roles, and Ability to Take Risks with Self.

A career development program based on this model was taught over a sixteen-week period at the University of Maryland, and was designed to measure the differential effects of three instructional approaches (developmental, traditional, and mixed). Most of the seventy-six participants were freshmen and sophomores. The developmental approach is based on the work of Widick, Knefelkamp, and Parker (1975), as discussed above. It is organized around Perry's theory of development and utilizes Sanford's (1966) concepts of support and challenge. The goals for the program were: (1) to teach content; (2) to help students relate ideas from the course to other areas of their lives; and (3) to expand the complexity of their thinking about career issues.

An instrument designed to assess students' complexity of thinking about careers as described in the Knefelkamp and Slepitza model was administered as a pre- and posttest and was used to determine Perry position score. The pretest results revealed that two thirds of the students entered the program in the dualistic positions (Positions 1–2), while one third entered at the multiplistic positions (Positions 3–4). The mean amount of stage movement for the developmental approach (.59) was much larger than that found using the other approaches.

Other studies of career development have extended the usefulness of the scheme to include the professional development of graduate students, in particular, those enrolled in master's or doctoral level student personnel programs. Mason (1978), Slepitza (1976), and Wertheimer (1976) have focused on establishing the validity of the Knefelkamp-Slepitza model. Mason (1978) studied changes in cognitive complexity, locus of control, and empathy among master's level counseling students who were enrolled in a year-long counseling course sequence which was taught using the methodology of developmental instruction. She found that statistically significant changes in development on each of these variables had occurred over the year-long period. These career development studies demonstrate that the usefulness of the Perry scheme in designing instructional programs is not limited to those with academic content, and that it can also be used to map a person's career and professional development as well. The generalizability of the scheme across many content areas is another reason for its power in understanding and explaining the diversity of experiences which constitute a college education.

critique

The small group of basic research studies reviewed here has in common the underlying purpose of determining the validity of the Perry scheme. It is difficult to draw a clear picture of the results from these studies, not because they are obviously contradictory or used with highly divergent samples, but because the variety of methods used to assess students' developmental levels calls into question the comparability of the obtained ratings. The assessment problem stands as the most critical concern facing subsequent research on the Perry scheme. Over eight different assessment procedures have been used to determine Perry position score, and to date, there has been no comprehensive attempt to cross-validate the measures in order to determine the comparability of position ratings assigned using these different procedures. Few if any psychometric properties of any of these procedures are known. Additionally, there is currently no standard set of rules used to rate the protocols from these various instruments, and learning to rate the protocols requires intensive training. Thus it is difficult for a researcher interested in the scheme to adequately judge, select, and use an assessment instrument.

In spite of the measurement problems, the evidence from the studies that have been conducted to date suggests that progression through the Perry positions does occur during college. However, very few examples of student ratings in the Committed positions have been found in any of the studies. It cannot be determined at this time if there actually are few students in the Committed positions, or if the instruments used are not successfully eliciting Committed responses.

It is striking that there has not yet been any major replication study of Perry's original research. The two major longitudinal studies now in progress (Clinchy and Zimmerman, 1975) and the two-year follow-up of King (1977) and Kitchener (1977) will help fill this void, but these results are not yet available for use in evaluating the validity of the theory by tracing movement through the positions over time.

Taken as a whole, however, the findings of the studies completed to date offer strong preliminary evidence for the validity of the Perry scheme. In spite of the preliminary nature of the empirical studies, it retains a strong degree of face validity: Many people can trace their own intellectual and ethical development through the scheme, recognizing themselves, their friends, or their students in the descriptions. Herein lies the explanatory power of the theory and the source of its usefulness in practice.

The applicability of the Perry scheme to design and conduct student development programs has been demonstrated in several intervention studies. What these studies offer in particular is the identification of environmental variables, variables over which the educational or developmental programmer has a degree of control and which can be structured to facilitate student development. For example, it has long been widely accepted that students have different needs and respond differentially to programs in which they are involved. The challenge to educators has been to "match" the programs to the needs of the students on important variables relevant to learning. However, consistently meeting students' immediate needs is not always an educationally sound strategy; there is value in "mismatch," or in creating an environment which challenges the student to adapt and respond in increasingly more adequate ways. As Widick and others (1975) suggest, however, the challenge of an educational environment must be coupled with the support of an educational community, lest it be too overwhelming to have a developmental influence.

Designing educational environments and programs which foster student development necessitates both the articulation of student development goals toward which the programs are directed, and a mapping of the process by which these goals are fulfilled. Perry's theory of the intellectual and ethical development of college students addresses both of these issues. The hierarchical nature of the scheme helps identify more adequate ways of reasoning about the outlining the steps necessary to reach the higher positions. With these resources inherent in the scheme, Perry's theory holds a great deal of promise for the student services practitioner, the researcher, and the administrator in achieving the common goal of the intentional promotion of student development.

references

Bieri, J. "Cognitive Structures in Personality." In H. Schroder and M. Suedfield (Eds.), *Personality Theory and Information Processing.* New York: Ronald Press, 1971.

Blake, L. "A Measure of Developmental Change: A Cross-Sectional Study." Paper presented at the annual meeting of the American Psychological Association, Washington, D.C., 1976.

Boyd, D. "Some Thoughts on a Comparison of Perry and Kohlberg." Unpublished manuscript, Harvard University, 1972.

Broughton, J. M. "The Development of Natural Epistemology in Adolescence and Early Adulthood." Unpublished doctoral dissertation, Harvard University, 1975.

Clinchy, B., Lief, J., and Young, P. "Epistemological and Moral Development in Girls from a Traditional and a Progressive High School." *Journal of Educational Psychology,* 1977, *69* (4), 337–343.

Clinchy, B., and Zimmerman, C. "Cognitive Development in College." Unpublished manuscript, Wellesley College, 1975.

Harvey, D. J., Hunt, D. E., and Schroder, H. M. *Conceptual Systems and Personality Organization.* New York: Wiley, 1961.

Heffernan, J. "Identity Formation, Identity Orientations and Sex Differences Related to College Environment Features: A Comparative Study of Conventional and Innovation Undergraduate Programs." Unpublished doctoral dissertation, University of Michigan, 1971.

King, P. M. "Taking a Stand With Yourself: Making Commitments in a Relativistic World." Unpublished manuscript, University of Minnesota, 1976.

King, P. M. "The Development of Reflective Judgment and Formal Operational Thinking in Adolescents and Young Adults." Unpublished doctoral dissertation, University of Minnesota, 1977.

Kitchener, K. S. "Intellectual Development in Late Adolescents and Young Adults: Reflective Judgment and Verbal Reasoning." Unpublished doctoral dissertation, University of Minnesota, 1977.

Kitchener, K. S., and King, P. M. "Intellectual Development Beyond Adolescence: Reflective Judgment, Formal Operations and Verbal Reasoning." Unpublished paper, forthcoming.

Knefelkamp, L. L. "Developmental Instruction: Fostering Intellectual and Personal Growth in College Students." Unpublished doctoral dissertation, University of Minnesota, 1974.

Knefelkamp, L. L. "The Knefelkamp/Slepitza Model of Career Development—A Relook at its Descriptive Stages." Unpublished manuscript, University of Maryland, 1978.

50

Knefelkamp, L. L., and Slepitza, R. L. "A Cognitive-Developmental Model of Career Development—An Adaptation of the Perry Scheme." *The Counseling Psychologist,* 1976, *6,* 53–58.

Kohlberg, L. "Stage and Sequence: The Cognitive-Developmental Approach to Socialization." In D. P. Goslin (Ed.), *Handbook of Socialization Theory and Research.* Chicago: Rand McNally, 1969.

Kohlberg, L. "From Is to Ought: How to Commit the Naturalistic Fallacy and Get Away with it in the Study of Moral Development." In T. Mischel (Ed.), *Cognitive Development and Epistemology.* New York: Academic Press, 1971.

Kohlberg, L. *Standard Scoring Manual, Form A.* Cambridge, Mass.: Harvard University, Moral Education Research Foundation, 1973.

Kurfiss, J. "Sequentiality and Structure in a Cognitive Model of College Student Development." *Developmental Psychology,* 1977, *13* (6), 565–571.

Loevinger, J. *Ego Development: Conception and Theories.* San Francisco: Jossey-Bass, 1976.

Mason, K. E. "Effects of Developmental Instruction on the Development of Cognitive Complexity, Locus of Control and Empathy in Beginning Counseling Graduate Students." Unpublished master's thesis, University of Maryland, 1978.

Maves, P. B. "Religious Development in Adulthood." In M. Strommen (Ed.), *Research on Religious Development.* New York: Hawthorn Books, 1971.

Meyer, P. "Intellectual Development of College Students as Measured by Analysis of Religious Content." Unpublished doctoral dissertation, University of Minnesota, 1975.

Meyer, P. "Intellectual Development: Analysis of Religious Content." *The Counseling Psychologist,* 1977, *6* (4), 47–50.

Perry, W. G., Jr. *Forms of Intellectual and Ethical Development in the College Years.* New York: Holt, Rinehart and Winston, 1970.

Rest, J. R. "Developmental Psychology as a Guide to Value Education: A Review of 'Kohlbergian' Programs." *Review of Educational Research,* 1973, *44* (2), 241–259.

Rest, J. R., Cooper, D., Coder, R., Masanz, J., and Anderson, D. "Judging the Important Issues in Moral Dilemmas." *Developmental Psychology,* 1974, *10* (4), 491–501.

Sanford, N. *Self and Society.* New York: Atherton Press, 1966.

Selman, R. L. *First Things: Social Reasoning.* New York: Guidance Associates, 1974.

Slepitza, R. L. "The Validation of Stage Model of Career Counseling." Unpublished master's thesis, University of Maryland, 1976.

Stephenson, B. W., and Hunt, C. "Intellectual and Ethical Development: A Dualistic Curriculum and Intervention for College Students." *The Counseling Psychologist,* 1977, *6,* 39–42.

Strange, C. C. "Intellectual Development, Motive for Education and Learning Styles During the College Years: A Comparison of Adult and Traditional-Age Students." Unpublished doctoral dissertation, University of Iowa, 1978.

Terman, L. M. *Concept Mastery Test: Manual.* New York: Psychological Corporation, 1973.

Touchton, J. G., Wertheimer, L. C., Cornfeld, J. L., and Harrison, K. H. "Career Planning and Decision-Making: A Developmental Approach to the Classroom." *The Counseling Psychologist,* 1977, *6* (4), 42–47.

Wertheimer, L. C. "A New Model and Measure for Career Counseling: Incorporating Both Content and Processing Aspects of Career Concerns." Unpublished master's thesis, University of Maryland, 1976.

Widick, C. C. "An Evaluation of Developmental Instruction in a University Setting." Unpublished doctoral dissertation, University of Minnesota, 1975.

Widick, C. C., Knefelkamp, L. L., and Parker, C. A. "The Counselor as a Developmental Instructor." *Counselor Education and Supervision,* 1975, 14, 286–296.

Patricia M. King is the senior research psychologist for the Division of Student Services, and is assistant professor in the Division of Educational Psychology, Measurement and Statistics at the University of Iowa. As Coordinator of the Iowa Student Development Project, she directs several research projects on issues related to student development and serves as a consultant in program development and evaluation for the Division of Student Services.

The college experience may be a very critical period for the development of moral reasoning because the student either will continue to hold to a conventional level of reasoning or be sufficiently jarred that he begins to question previously unquestioned beliefs.

Lawrence Kohlberg's cognitive stage theory of the development of moral judgment

alexander f. smith

Kohlberg, in his largely intuitive and theoretical model of moral development, has built on the ideas of Dewey (1939) and Piaget (1965). Dewey had conceptualized three levels of moral development (premoral, conventional, and autonomous). It was Dewey's belief that value and moral considerations were an important concern of the educational curriculum and that development was a legitimate aim of education. Piaget, after watching children at play in a game of marbles and by observing their attitude toward rules and authority, proposed basically a two-stage theory of moral development. The first stage, which Piaget called the *stage of heteronomy,* was based on a "morality of constraint." The second stage, a more mature stage based on a "morality of cooperation," was called the *stage of autonomy.*

For his dissertation study at the University of Chicago, Kohlberg (1958) attempted to validate Dewey's and Piaget's assumptions about stages of development in his study of the moral development of fifty boys between the ages of ten and sixteen. Based on this dissertation study and further research, Kohlberg advanced and delineated the differences in stages of moral growth suggested by Dewey and Piaget, particularly by identifying and describing an adult level of moral reasoning, based on moral principles, also influenced by the work of Rawls (1971) at Harvard University.

Kohlberg's research identified three general levels of moral thought, with each level consisting of two stages, so that in all he identified six stages of moral reasoning. His research is concerned with identifying the qualitiatively different modes of moral reasoning or moral judgment that make up each of the different levels and stages of moral thought. As such, this theory is appropriately labeled a cognitive-developmental theory. It also can best be described as a theory about the development of moral judgment or moral reasoning.

Currently Kohlberg serves as director of Harvard's Center for Moral Education, where he is working to improve his methods of assessing moral reasoning and to further refine and define his descriptions of the stages of moral development. He also is applying his theory of moral development through several moral development projects, one of which involves a Boston high school.

theory

Concept of Cognitive Stage Development. The central concept in this theory is that of *stages* of moral development. Moral judgment is described as proceeding through various stages of development. A moral stage represents a mode or structure of thought. Each stage is qualitatively different in its structure from other stages. When determining what that structure is, one is concerned with how the judgments are made; the "whys," not the "whats," or the "content" of the judgment. The structure of moral thought includes such components as the rule or decision-making system, the problem-solving strategy, the social perspective, and the underlying logic employed in making a moral choice.

The cognitive-development theory holds also that the stages of moral development are universal. The basic structure of thought that differentiates one stage from another will be found in other cultures, too; whereas the so-called "content" of each stage represents the various values that a person holds. These values are relative and may be culturally or socially determined, but the basic structure of each stage is not culturally determined. Kohlberg's use of the stage construct follows that of Piaget.

Description of Stages of Moral Development. From his empirical investigation of the judgments that the boys in his sample made in response to hypothetical moral dilemmas, Kohlberg (1971b) identified six stages of moral development:

I. Preconventional Level

At this level the child is responsive to cultural rules and labels of good and bad, right and wrong, but interprets these labels either in terms of the physical or the hedonistic consequences of action (punishment, reward, exchange of favors) or in terms of the physical power of those who enunciate the rules and labels. The level is divided into the following two stages:

Stage 1: The Punishment-and-Obedience Orientation. The physical consequences of action determine its goodness or badness, regardless of the human meaning or values of these consequences. Avoidance of punishment and unquestioning deference to power are valued in their own right, not in terms of respect for an underlying moral order supported by punishment and authority (the latter being Stage 4).

Stage 2: The Instrumental-Relativist Orientation. Right action consists of that which instrumentally satisfies one's own needs and occasionally the needs of others. Human relations are viewed in terms like those of the market place. Elements of fairness, of reciprocity, and of equal sharing are present, but they are always interpreted in a physically pragmatic way. Reciprocity is a matter of "you scratch my back and I'll scratch yours," not of loyalty, gratitude, or justice.

II. Conventional Level

At this level, maintaining the expectations of the individual's family, group, or nation is perceived as valuable in its own right, regardless of immediate and obvious consequences. The attitude is not only one of *conformity* to personal expectations and social order, but of loyalty to it, of actively *maintaining,* supporting, and justifying the order, and of identifying with the persons or group involved in it. At this level, there are the following two stages:

Stage 3: The Interpersonal Concordance or "Good Boy— Nice Girl" Orientation. Good behavior is that which pleases or helps others and is approved by them. There is much conformity to stereotypical images of what is majority or "natural" behavior. Behavior is frequently judged by intention—"he means well" becomes important for the first time. One earns approval by being "nice."

Stage 4: The "Law and Order" Orientation. There is orientation toward authority, fixed rules, and the maintenance of the social order. Right behavior consists of doing one's duty, showing respect for authority, and maintaining the given social order for its own sake.

III. Postconventional, Autonomous, or Principled Level

At this level, there is a clear effort to define moral values and principles that have validity and application apart from the authority of the groups or persons holding these principles and apart from the individual's own identification with these groups. This level again has two stages:

Stage 5: The Social Contract, Legalistic Orientation, Generally with Utilitarian Overtones. Right action tends to be defined in terms of general individual rights, and standards which have been critically examined and agreed upon by the whole society. There is a clear awareness of the relativism of personal values and opinions and a corresponding emphasis on procedural rules for reaching consensus. Aside from what is constitutionally and democratically agreed upon, the right is a matter of personal "values" and "opinion." The result is an emphasis on the "legal point of view," but with an emphasis on the possibility of changing law in terms of rational considerations of social utility (rather than freezing it in terms of Stage 4 "law and order"). Outside the legal realm, free agreement and contract are the binding elements of obligation. This is the "official" morality of the American government and constitution.

Stage 6. The Universal-Ethical-Principle Orientation. Right is defined by the decision of conscience in accord with self-chosen *ethical principles* appealing to logical comprehensiveness, universality, and consistency. These principles are abstract and ethical (the Golden Rule, the categorical imperative); they are not concrete moral rules like the Ten Commandments. At heart, these are universal principles of *justice,* of the *reciprocity* and *equality* of human rights, and of respect for the dignity of human beings as *individual* persons (Kohlberg, 1971b).

Two major concepts or themes are reflected in Kohlberg's description of the stages of moral judgment. These are the concept of empathy or role taking and the concept of justice. The various stages of moral development can be distinguished by the manner in which these concepts are applied. Role taking is the ability to view situations from another person's perspective. Unless one can realize the existence of different perspectives, a moral conflict cannot even arise.

Each stage of moral reasoning reflects, according to the theory, a different basis for deciding what is the *just* or *fair* or *right* way to resolve a moral dilemma. At the preconventional level, it is the personal consequences of an act or decision which are the basis for deciding right and wrong. Stealing is wrong, for example, because one might be suspended from school or arrested. At the conventional level, what is *just* is determined by the laws or conventions of society. Stealing is wrong because it is against the law. At the postconventional level, what is *just* is no longer based on a specific prescriptive set of rules but on abstract moral principles that can be applied to many situations. At this level stealing might be described as wrong because it is wrong to take someone else's property without permission (a recognition of the property rights of others) or, in the classic Heinz (Rest, 1974a) moral dilemma, that it may be right to steal a drug because the value placed on saving a life is more important than protecting property. Equity—the need to treat everyone equally—is the principle of justice expressed at the highest stage of moral development.

The Invariant Sequence of Moral Development. To develop morally is to move through each stage (starting with the least differentiated), one by one in sequence. A person does not move from a Stage Two level of moral reasoning to a Stage Four level of moral reasoning without first passing through Stage Three. According to the theory of cognitive development, this order of progression never varies. Not everyone will move at the same rate through these stages, and not everyone will advance to the highest level of moral development. In fact, Kohlberg's (1969) research suggested that only about 20-25 percent of the adult population will reach the most mature levels of moral development.

Necessary Conditions for Moral Development. Higher stages of moral development demand the ability to see perspectives other than one's own. Thus the development of role taking ability is a necessary process if the full development of moral reasoning is to occur. The ability to reason logically and to use formal operations is also necessary. Moral reasoning has a strong cognitive core. Understanding and using higher forms of moral reasoning requires the ability, in Piagetian terms, to be at a formal operation stage. The level of moral reasoning will not surpass the general level of cognitive reasoning. On the other hand, moral reasoning does not necessarily reach its optimum level and may lag behind cognitive development.

Process of Moral Development and Role of Environment. Development of moral judgment, according to Kohlberg (1972), is the result of an increasing ability to organize and integrate social experience. The cognitive-developmental view holds that growth in moral reasoning occurs naturally as the result of continuous interaction between an individual and the environment. Opportunities created in the environment to role play, to be confronted by different social or moral perspectives, to have the opportunity to make decisions and discuss moral or ethical issues all serve to stimulate the development of moral reasoning. The absence of those opportunities removes that stimulation and may retard development. If the cognitive development has not reached the level of development to handle increasing complexity of information and reasoning required by a more advanced stage of moral development, development to that next stage will not take place. The movement through stages takes appropriate experiences and time before an individual is ready to move on. This process of filling out a stage, acquiring a readiness to move on, has been referred to as *horizontal decalage* (Rest, 1973).

Since each stage represents an equilibrium or balancing point at which an individual's mode of structuring his perception of the social environment is stabilized, that structure needs to be challenged if development to the next stage is to occur. Creating a sufficient cognitive conflict or challenge to create structural disequilibrium is necessary for development. Too much conflict, on the other hand, may create a situation that would retard development.

Transition to an Adult Stage of Moral Reasoning. Moral reasoning during the early college years appeared to reflect a period of regression in moral thinking. In a longitudinal study, Kramer (1968), found a downward shift in level of moral reasoning of many who were at Stage 4 during late high school to a Stage 2 level of moral thinking during the early college years. Several years later these same individuals had advanced to Stage 5. A similar phenomenon was reported by Haan, Smith, and Block (1968) in their study of college students in the San Francisco Bay area. This reported phenomenon of regression was in direct contradiction to the notion of an invariant sequence of stage progression.

However, work by Turiel (1974), who interviewed groups of high school students and college undergraduates, helped to formulate the idea of a period of transitional moral thinking among some college students which might account for this regression in moral thinking. In his study, Turiel (p. 13) found that a number of subjects made ambiguous judgments characterized by inconsistency, conflict, and internal contradiction. Students in these situations seemed to deny morality and to typically state that: (1) all values are relative and arbitrary; (2) one should not judge what another person should do; (3) it is up to every individual to make his own decisions; and (4) terms like duty, good, should, or moral have no meaning. Turiel did find that on some issues students did take a moral position. He believed that this simultaneous denial of morality and the presence of some moral assertion was characteristic of the transition process in which some partial rejection of Stage 4 conceptions does take place.

Results from other studies (Rest, 1974b) indicate that the predominant mode of thinking among college students in general is conventional reasoning of a Stage 3 or Stage 4 type. A smaller number of students enter a period of transition from a conventional to a principled form of moral reasoning. During this phase, their moral reasoning may appear relativistic, inconsistent, or possibly antiauthoritarian. An even smaller number of college students actually reach a level of consistent principled thinking (Stage 5 or 6).

This suggests that the college experience may be a very critical period for the development of moral reasoning. Either a student will continue to hold to a conventional level of reasoning, with the college experience elaborating or solidifying that level of reasoning; or a student's conventional form of reasoning may be sufficiently jarred that the student begins to question previously unquestioned beliefs and expands the range or level of consideration of moral issues. Students who enter this transitional phase may struggle for quite some time before they establish a more mature set of moral principles. If a major shift in the structure of moral reasoning is to occur, the college setting has the potential power to stimulate this shift.

In the initial construction of the theory it was the belief that adult moral development was only a continuous development toward more stability and consistency in moral reasoning: "Adult moral development was primarily a matter of dropping out of childish modes of thought rather than the formation of new or higher modes of thought. . . . The major change in moral thought past high school is a significant increase or stabilization of conventional morality of a stage 4 variety, at the expense of preconventional stage of thought" (Kohlberg, 1973a, p. 106). Recent research (Gilligan and Kohlberg, 1974; Kohlberg, 1973b) now supports the conclusion that there is a distinctive form of adult thinking. It is represented by a movement toward postconventional or principled thinking (Stage 5). When Kohlberg rescored his data, he found that none of his subjects displayed true Stage 5 thinking under the age of twenty-three.

assessment of moral reasoning

Two methods have been developed to assess stage or moral reasoning. Both methods utilize hypothetical moral dilemmas that require the respondent to make judgments. An example of one such dilemma follows:

> In Europe, a woman was near death from a very bad disease, a special kind of cancer. There was one drug that the doctors thought might save her. It was a form of radium that a druggist in the same town had recently discovered. The drug was expensive to make, but the druggist was charging ten times what the drug cost him to make. He paid $200 for the radium and charged $2000 for a small dose of the drug. The sick woman's

husband, Heinz, went to everyone he knew to borrow the money, but he could get together about $1000 which was half what it cost. He told the druggist that his wife was dying, and asked him to sell it cheaper or let him pay for it later. But the druggist said, "No, I discovered the drug and I'm going to make money from it." Heinz got desperate and broke into the man's store to steal the drug for his wife. (Kohlberg, 1973a, p. 157)

Kohlberg and his associates at Harvard developed a scoring system to rate the responses made to a series of questions that follows each dilemma such as: Should Heinz have done that? Was it right or wrong? Responses are rated by judges according to the stage of reasoning reflected by the response. Scores from the ratings of responses to the individual dilemmas are summed to provide a global moral maturity score and a stage score.

Rest (1974c) and his colleagues at the University of Minnesota have developed an objective instrument that is based on Kohlberg's stage conception called the *Defining Issues Test* (DIT) to assess moral development. This instrument consists of six hypothetical moral dilemmas. Each dilemma is followed by twelve issue statements that reflect different stages of moral judgment. The respondent first rates these issues in terms of importance and then ranks the top four issues which are most important in deciding the issue. The scoring system developed for this instrument provides an objective measure of principled thinking and of stage type based on the respondents' ranking of issues following each story.

research

The research that has been conducted has tended to support the hierarchical and universal properties of stage structure described by Kohlberg. Research also has supported the notion that development proceeds through a sequence of stages.

Kohlberg and Gilligan (1971) in a cross-cultural study of middle-class urban boys in the United States, Taiwan, and Mexico reported that progression of stage usage followed the same order in each culture. Kohlberg and Kramer (1969) conducted a study in two isolated villages, one in Turkey and the other in Yucatan, that showed the same pattern of development. They found increasing usage of Stage 3 and Stage 4 thinking and a decrease in Stage 1 and Stage 2 usage with age. The degree of development reported in other cultures is not as rapid as it is in the United States, but the sequence and direction of stage development appears to be the same.

Additional support for the hierarchical nature of stage development and for the idea that each higher stage represents a more adequate way of reasoning than the previous stage comes from a study by Rest, Turiel, and Kohlberg (1969). They tested the preference for and the comprehension of stage reasoning for one stage below, and for one and two stages above, the level of the subjects participating in this study. They found that the subjects, when presented with examples of different stage reasoning, preferred the higher stage reasoning to lower reasoning. However, the subjects' comprehension decreased as stage level increased. In another study Rest (1973) reported that subjects comprehended reasoning up to one stage above their own level of reasoning. In an effort to discover if subjects can fake their response to reflect higher levels of reasoning, McGeorge (1975) found that subjects could fake down but could not fake up.

Holstein (1976) followed the development of moral judgment for fifty-two adolescents and their parents longitudinally over a three-year period. She found evidence for a step- and time-related sequence of the development from the preconventional to the conventional level of moral judgment. However, at the higher stages Holstein found some evidence of regression in stage thinking as did Kramer (1968) in an earlier study. Holstein also found evidence of sex bias in the scoring system developed by Kohlberg. Women in her study scored lower on issues of affection than did the men. Gilligan (1977) also has reported her concern that Kohlberg's scoring system favors men.

Turiel (1974, 1977) conducted one of the few studies of the process of structural reorganization which accounts for stage movement. In his longitudinal study of adolescents, Turiel found that those subjects initially determined to be in transition were marked by conflict and inconsistencies in their moral reasoning. A year and a half later these same subjects were at a Stage 5 level of reasoning and their reasoning no longer reflected those inconsistencies. Only those subjects who were in a transitional phase from conventional to postconventional reasoning advanced to postconventional reasoning. The transitional period was described by Turiel as one of disequilibrium or conflict in moral reasoning. The resolution of that disequilibrium came through a structural reorganization represented by Stage 5 level of moral reasoning.

Rest, Davison, and Robbins (1978) recently completed a review of cross-sectional data collected on several thousand high school, college, and graduate students from across the United States, using Rest's (1974c) *Defining Issues Test* (DIT). They found support for the general model of moral development proposed by Kohlberg. When they reanalyzed the data from these studies, they found that there was an increase in higher stage usage and a decrease in lower stage usage. These studies also support the claim for a postconventional level of moral reasoning. One of the most significant findings reported from this large data pool was that high school and college students showed the most dramatic change or shift in moral development. If students leave school they tend to plateau in moral judgment development; but students who continue on to graduate or professional school continue to make gains.

Experimental efforts show that it is possible to increase the level of moral reasoning. Blatt and Kohlberg (1975) were successful in increasing level of moral judgment through classroom moral discussion. Rest and others (1978) in their review of data from numerous studies that used the *Defining Issues Test* report that "studies of experimentally induced change show that DIT scores can be significantly increased by moral education interventions of several months' duration, but not by short-term interventions" (p. 277).

Few studies have directly examined the relationship between moral judgment and moral behavior, although Kohlberg (1975b) has claimed that moral judgment is the single most important variable in explaining moral behavior. Krebbs and Rosenwald (1977) reported that significantly fewer principled stage subjects cheated during a contrived cheating study. Kohlberg (1975a) has stated that when the responses of the Watergate defendants were analyzed, none of the responses were even above a Stage 4 level of reasoning. Smith (1978) studied the level of moral reasoning of students involved in campus discipline infractions. He found that most of the violators were at a conventional level of moral reasoning, and that few violators had reached a principled or postconventional level.

analysis and implications for practice

Late adolescence and young adulthood is a critical time in the process of moral development, as the results of research have indicated. Most college-age students are at a conventional Stage 3 or 4. A few students are in a transitional phase from conventional to postconventional moral reasoning. The collegiate experience has the potential to make a significant difference in whether a student stabilizes his moral thinking or moves successfully from conventional to postconventional thought.

Kohlberg's theory is concerned only with the development of moral judgment. Its rather detailed description and analysis of the moral reasoning of the adult and young adult, however, makes it useful in understanding at least one aspect of college student development. The process of sequential stage development and the importance placed on social experience in providing a stimulus for moral development provide important guides for developing programs.

Both Dewey (1909) and Kohlberg (1972) have pointed out that experience in confronting moral issues or questions is imperative if moral development is to occur. If the college experience is to affect moral development, there must be opportunities that will enable students to actively experience different levels of moral reasoning and to make moral judgments. To the extent that the students' social experience is a laboratory in which they can test their judgment, reflect on their behavior, and engage in informal discussions with their peers, instructors or advisors, the development of more mature forms of moral thought can occur.

Informal interactive experiences do lead to further moral development. However, by accepting a broader educational responsibility, particularly in the out-of-classroom environment of the student, the student personnel worker can have a much more intentional role as a facilitator of development. The opportunity to interact with students either through formal structures such as committees or student government groups, for example, or informally as advisors or counselors already exists. Kohlberg's cognitive stage theory of development in its analysis of stage level reasoning and description of the stepwise nature of development provides direction for practice. Some programs and applications of this theory in the college setting are discussed below.

Moral education programs in the classroom have been one of the first and most frequent ways to implement cognitive-stage theory concepts. Such programs have included: the use and discussion of hypothetical moral dilemmas, the study of women characters in novels and plays and the moral issues confronted in the plot, readings and discussions of moral philosophers, and the direct teaching of stage concepts as part of a developmental psychology course (Rest, 1974a). A classroom format may involve the instructor modeling +1 stage reasoning or the use of readings and discussions which will involve students with different levels of moral judgment.

Kohlberg (1975a) has suggested that moral development can be stimulated by the discussion method when there is: (1) exposure to the next highest level of moral reasoning; (2) exposure to stimulus that poses conflict or contradiction in current modes of moral reasoning; and (3) an open atmosphere for dialogue in which conflicting moral views can be compared. The discussion method, however, need not be restricted to formal classroom use. Special programs can be designed for use in community living situations, such as residence halls and fraternity houses. Campus leadership training programs, particularly when focused on moral leadership, can also use such a format. Moral dilemmas or situations used as part of such programs can come from the real life experience of the individuals or of the group and might include such topics as: abortion, termination of or initiating relationships, premarital sex, cheating in the classroom, fudging information on a financial aid form, student suicides, and drug abuse.

Cognitive-developmental theory also provides strong endorsement for the involvement of students in campus life programs and in student government or other decision-making related activities. When students have the opportunity to participate in various types of group decisions or discussions, they are exposed to different levels of judgment and see their own reasoning as a subject for discussion or reaction. When the groups are diverse in membership and include adult participants such as faculty and staff, there is a greater likelihood that some students will be exposed to a level of reasoning that exceeds their own. Obviously, not all groups or committees are involved with decisions or issues that have an underlying moral dimension, but some do. Judicial boards are one example. So are certain groups or committees which make decisions or recommendations on the allocation of resources or on major policy decisions affecting people in different ways. These formal structures are a ready means for discussion and dialogue. When appropriate, the moral considerations can be discussed; this provides another opportunity for students to be faced with moral issues.

Campus discipline is another area of student personnel practice where cognitive-developmental theory can play an important role in practice. Certain behavior such as theft, destruction of property, and cheating have moral implications. Staff members conducting discipline interviews and properly trained judicial board members can help to challenge less mature forms of moral reasoning and model a higher stage level of moral judgment. One objective for a campus discipline program might be to provide experiences of discipline processes consistent with the stimulation of moral development.

Knowledge and use of stage theory is also important in the effective communication of campus policies and regulations. How such information is expressed and interpreted can be consistent with moral development. Rest (1973) has reported that students can comprehend all stages of moral development up to and including their own stage, but do not comprehend stages of moral reasoning more than one stage above their own. Matching a response to the student's own level of moral reasoning, or to the next level, can be an effective intervention strategy. Advisors, counselors, and administrators working with individual students or student groups can apply that understanding of stage structure to their work.

Staff development and paraprofessional training programs are another important area of application for this theory. If student personnel practitioners are representative of the adult population in general, only a certain percentage will reason at a principled level of moral thought. The moral development of some students will exceed that of some educators and administrative staff members, which will make it difficult for student personnel to match their level of response with that of the students and to function effectively as facilitators. This makes the moral development of student personnel workers and paraprofessionals a matter of concern for professional and staff development.

The use of moral discussion and the introduction of moral development concepts in training programs, staff and professional development experiences, and in the graduate curriculum can lead to a higher level of moral reasoning and moral behavior in the profession and enable more individuals at both the professional and paraprofessional levels to actively and intentionally function in ways that can facilitate the moral development of college students.

references

Baltes, P. B., and Schaie, K. W. (Eds.). *Life-Span Developmental Psychology: Personality and Socialization.* New York: Academic press, 1973.

Beck, C. M., Crittenden, B. S., and Sullivan, E. V. *Moral Education: Interdisciplinary Approaches.* New York: Paulist Press, 1971. (Also Toronto: University of Toronto Press, 1971.)

Blatt, M., and Kohlberg, L. "The Effects of Classroom Moral Discussion upon Children's Level of Moral Judgment." *Journal of Moral Education,* 1975, *4* (2), 129-161. (Also available in L. Kohlberg. *Collected Papers on Moral Development and Moral Education.* Cambridge: Moral Education Research Foundation, 1973.)

DePalma, D. J., and Foley, J. M. *Moral Development: Current Theory and Research.* New Jersey: Lawrence Erlbaum Associates, 1975.

Dewey, J. *Moral Principles in Education.* New York: Houghton Mifflin, 1909.

Dewey, J. *Theory of Valuation.* Chicago: University of Chicago Press, 1939.

Duska, R., and Whelan, M. *Moral Development: A Guide to Piaget and Kohlberg.* Paramus: Paulist-Newman Press, 1975.

Gibbs, T. C. "Kohlberg's Stages of Moral Judgment: A Constructive Critique." *Harvard Educational Review,* 1977, *47,* 43-61.

Gilligan, C. "In a Different Voice: Women's Conception of Self and Morality." *Harvard Educational Review,* 1977, *47,* 481-517.

Gilligan, C., and Kohlberg, L. "From Adolescent to Adulthood: The Rediscovery of Reality in a Post-Conventional World." Paper given at annual meeting of Jean Piaget Society, June 1974.

Haan, N., Smith, M. B., and Block, J. "The Moral Reasoning of Young Adults: Political-Social Behavior, Family Background, and Personality Correlates." *Journal of Personality and Social Psychology,* 1968, *10* (3), 183-201.

Holstein, C. B. "Irreversible, Stepwise Sequence in the Development of Moral Judgment: A Longitudinal Study of Males and Females." *Child Development,* 1976, *47,* 51-61.

Kohlberg, L. "The Development of Modes of Moral Thinking and Choice in the Years Ten to Sixteen." Unpublished doctoral dissertation, University of Chicago, 1958.

Kohlberg, L. "Moral Education in the Schools: A Developmental View." *The School Review,* 1966, *74,* 1-30.

Kohlberg, L. "Stage and Sequence: The Cognitive Developmental Approach to Socialization." In D. Goslin (Ed.), *Handbook of Socialization Theory and Research.* Chicago: Rand McNally, 1969.

Kohlberg, L. "From is to Ought: How to Commit the Naturalistic Fallacy and Get Away with it in the Study of Moral Development." In T. Mischel (Ed.), *Cognitive Development and Epistemology.* New York: Academic Press, 1971a.

Kohlberg, L. "Stages of Moral Development." In C. M. Beck, B. S. Crittenden, and E. V. Sullivan (Eds.), *Moral Education.* Toronto: University of Toronto Press, 1971b.

Kohlberg, L. *Collected Papers on Moral Development and Moral Education.* Cambridge: Moral Education Research Foundation, Harvard University Graduate School of Education, 1973a.

Kohlberg, L. "Continuities in Childhood and Adult Moral Development Revisited." In P. B. Baltes and K. W. Schaie (Eds.), *Life-Span Developmental Psychology: Personality and Socialization.* New York: Academic Press, 1973b.

Kohlberg, L. "A Cognitive Developmental Approach to Moral Education." *Humanist,* 1972, *6,* 13-16.

Kohlberg, L. "The Cognitive-Developmental Approach to Moral Education." *Phi Delta Kappan,* 1975a, *56* (1), 670-677.

Kohlberg, L. "Moral Education for a Society in Moral Transition." *Educational Leadership,* 1975b, *33* (1), 46-54.

Kohlberg, L., and Gilligan, C. "The Adolescent as a Philosopher: The Discovery of the Self in a Post-Conventional World." *Daedalus,* 1971, *100* (4), 1051-1086.

Kohlberg, L., and Kramer, R. "Continuities and Discontinuities in Childhood and Adult Moral Development." *Human Development,* 1969, *12* (2), 93-120.

Kohlberg, L., and Mayer, R. "Development as the Aim of Moral Education." *Harvard Educational Review,* 1972, *42* (4), 449-496.

Kohlberg, L., and Turiel, E. "Moral Development and Moral Education." In G. Lesser (Ed.), *Psychology and Educational Practice.* Chicago: Scott Foresman, 1971.

Kramer, R. "Moral Development in Young Adulthood." Unpublished doctoral dissertation, University of Chicago, 1968.

Krebbs, D., and Rosenwald, A. "Moral Reasoning and Moral Behavior in Conventional Adults." *Merrill-Palmer Quarterly,* 1977, *23,* 77-87.

Kurtines, W., and Grief, E. B. "The Development of Moral Thought: Review and Evaluation of Kohlberg's Approach." *Psychological Bulletin,* 1974, *81,* 453-470.

Lickona, T. (Ed.). *Moral Development and Behavior: Theory, Research, and Social Issues.* New York: Holt, Rinehart, and Winston, 1976.

McGeorge, C. "Susceptibility to Faking of Defining Issues Test of Moral Development." *Developmental Psychology,* 1975, *11* (1), 108.

Rawls, J. *A Theory of Justice.* Cambridge, Mass.: Harvard University Press, 1971.

Rest, J. R. "The Hierarchical Nature of Stages of Moral Judgment." *Journal of Personality,* 1973, *41* (1), 86-109.

Rest, J. R. "The Cognitive-Developmental Approach to Morality: The State of the Art." *Counseling and Values,* 1974a, *18* (2), 64-78.

Rest, J. R. "Developmental Psychology as a Guide to Value Education: A Review of 'Kohlbergian' Programs." *Review of Educational Research,* 1974b, *44* (2), 241-259.

Rest, J. R. *Manual for the Defining Issues Test.* Minneapolis: Minnesota Moral Research Projects, University of Minnesota, 1974c.

Rest, J. R. "Longitudinal Study of the Defining Issues Test of Moral Judgment: A Strategy for Analyzing Developmental Change." *Developmental Psychology,* 1975, *11* (6), 738-748.

Rest, J., Turiel, E., and Kohlberg, L. "Level of Moral Development as a Determinant of Preference and Comprehension of Moral Judgments Made by Others." *Journal of Personality,* 1969, *37,* 225-252.

Smith, A. F. "Developmental Issues and Themes in the Discipline Setting—Suggestions for Educational Practice." Unpublished doctoral dissertation, Ohio State University, 1978.

Straub, C. A. "A Developmental Approach to Education: Fostering Autonomy in College Women." Unpublished master's thesis, Ohio State University, 1978.

Turiel, E. "Stage Transition in Moral Development." In R. M. Travers (Ed.), *Second Handbook of Research on Teaching.* Chicago: Rand McNally, 1973.

Turiel, E. "Conflict and Transition in Adolescent Moral Development." *Child Development,* 1974, *45* (1), 14.

Turiel, E. "Conflict and Transition in Adolescent Moral Development, II: The Resolution of Disequilibrium Through Structural Reorganization." *Child Development,* 1977, *48,* 634–637.

Turiel, E. "Comparative Analysis of Moral Knowledge and Moral Judgment in Males and Females." *Journal of Personality,* 1976, *44* (2), 195–209.

Alexander F. Smith is a student personnel practitioner.
He is associate dean of students for student
programming at Wittenberg University in
Springfield, Ohio.

*The work of Loevinger provides an integrated model
of human development and her unique methodology
suggests specific ways to study the developmental process.*

Jane Loevinger's milestones of development

lee knefelkamp
clyde a. parker
carole widick

Loevinger and Wessler's model of ego development differs somewhat from the other developmental models we have reviewed: (1) the model is not based directly upon studies of college students, but rather on heterogeneous groups of women spanning wide differences in age (10-over 50), race, education, and employment status; (2) the model was originally developed for women and girls and only later applied to men; and (3) the model is a result of empirical data collected using the Sentence Completion Test (Loevinger and Wessler, 1970a) and did not grow out of a practitioner's work with and observations of college students. The decision to include Loevinger was based on two important considerations: her work is an important integrating model of human development and her methodology suggests specific ways of studying the developmental process. While primarily a cognitive stage theorist, her work encompasses interpersonal relationships, moral and ethical development, and cognitive complexity. The study of ego development has two complementary but distinct aspects; it is both:

1. the study of "the course of character development within the individual" (Loevinger, 1976, p. 3), and
2. a formal discipline, a "way of doing psychology as science" (Loevinger, 1976, p. xiii).

While her work offers a definite perspective on how to study the complexity of ego development, it does not speak directly to practitioners about use of the model with students. As a consequence, we have chosen to accentuate her contributions as a model builder and a research methodologist rather than the programmatic implications of her work.

the concept of ego development

Loevinger's work conceptualizes the individual as a dynamic and unified being who has the capacity to interpret and act on his physical, social, and psychological environment. The individual is seen as a coherent whole, one in which "many diverse aspects of thought, interpersonal relationships, impulse control, and character grow at once, in some more or less coherent way" (1976, p. ix).

Critical to Loevinger's understanding of *how* the individual can interpret and act on the world are the concepts of structure and the ego. The ego is the central element of the self which "provides the frame of reference. . . . within which one perceives the world" (1976, p. 9). Loevinger relies on the structural assumptions of cognitive developmental theory as a "central theme" (1976, p. x) of her work and defines the ego's "frame of reference" as "structure." For Loevinger the term structure implies "that there are many elements or parts and that these elements are not simply an aggregate, an assemblage, as in a heap of stones, but are related to each other in a well defined order" (1976, p. 32). The individual's structure determines how he interacts with the environment by a) selecting what he will respond to and b) by choosing a response that accommodates the varying demands of different environments. Development is promoted by this interaction between the individual and the environment; thus development consists of acquiring a new structure or the change from an old structure to a new one. The individual's developmental progress is one of a series of transformations of structures from less to more complex.

These critical concepts place Loevinger's work in the family of stage theorists, primarily cognitive theorists, although Loevinger insists that ego development is the "master trait," one that encompasses the multiple facts of moral development, development of cognitive complexity, and development of the capacity for interpersonal relationships. Ego development symbolizes the whole of the person that is greater than the sum of its separate parts.

description of the model

Loevinger's model of ego development first appeared in print in 1966 and was refined by Loevinger and Wessler in their 1970 volume on the measurement of ego development. The latest Loevinger work (1976) contains a much expanded discussion of the stages and their characteristics. Our description of the model is based on all three primary sources which together define the following as characteristics of the model.

1. The individual is seen as a functioning whole who interacts with the world utilizing a series of ego structures.
2. "Stages" are "milestones" along a structure continuum from simplistic to complex.
3. "Stages" can be used to descriptively define where a person is along the continuum and thus serve as "types."
4. There is an inner logic to the structure of the stages and their progression. They exist in an irreversible, invariant, and hierarchical sequence. One cannot skip stages in the progression.
5. Each stage builds on the previous one and prepares and previews the following one.
6. Upward movement along the developmental continuum represents qualitative differences in the way the ego interacts with the environment.
7. The ego naturally seeks equilibrium and is prompted to develop more complex structures by interaction with an environmental condition that demands more complexity.
8. The model is applicable to all ages because age and stage are not perfectly correlated.
9. There exist specific research methods and assessment instruments that can help us advance our knowledge of ego development as defined in the model.

In its present form the model consists of ten stages. Loevinger urges us to refer to the stages by their name and not by a number because she assumes that continued research may produce the discovery of additional stages that current research techniques are not sophisticated enough to define. She reminds us that the original model consisted of only four stages and that now there are ten. We are also reminded that "although stage names suggest characteristics that are usually at a maximum at that stage, nothing less than the total pattern defines a stage" (1976, p. 15).

Presocial Stage. This stage reflects the individual before he has learned to differentiate himself from his surroundings. The young infant is not conceptualized as having an ego until he is able to accomplish the task of differentiation.

Symbiotic Stage. This stage is characterized by the symbiotic relationship between the infant and whoever plays the primary nurturing role in his life. The child is not differentiated from that primary person. Loevinger discusses the fact that these first two stages are not accessible by means of language in later life as are the remnants of all the later stages and hypothesizes that learning to use language enables the child to see himself as a separate person.

Impulsive Stage. During this stage the child is able to affirm his own identity as separate from others. The need for others remains strong and is characterized by demanding and dependent behavior patterns. The child is preoccupied with bodily impulses. Others in the social environment are seen as sources of reward or punishment and are classified as good or bad in terms of their treatment of him. The child is present oriented and does not conceptualize past or future very well, nor can he conceptualize himself as a causal agent.

Self-Protective Stage. During this stage the child begins to learn to control his impulses. He is able to conceptualize the relationship of his actions to short-term rewards and punishments and thus is newly and consciously vulnerable. While he sees *actions* related to reward or punishment, he is not yet able to accept responsibility for the fact that they are *his* actions. He is likely to place blame on some external factor or person. The individual can understand that rules exist, but the primary rule is really "don't get caught" for it is getting caught that defines an action as wrong. At this point in the model Loevinger first mentions the fact that older children and adults may remain at this stage level and are characterized as opportunistic and hedonistic if they do.

Conformist Stage. The individual now begins to identify his own welfare with that of the group—often the family or close peers. Loevinger states that this stage cannot be fully realized if the individual is lacking in basic trust of others. If this trust is lacking, the person is likely to remain at the Self-Protective level and exploit others for his own gain. The Conformist fears disapproval of the esteemed group and hence obeys its rules simply to conform and be approved. He still does not conceptualize ownership of responsibility for the consequences of his actions. The conforming personality perceives his group's norms and is thus insensitive to and unaccepting of individual differences. These individuals are prone to the use of stereotypes with respect to those who are different from themselves. Conformists value behaviors that preserve the group such as niceness, cooperation, and helpfulness, and tend to be less competitive than those at the Self-Protective stage. More than anything else, the Conformist seeks to belong; hence his behavior, goals, interests—often his very appearance—are externally influenced and controlled. Loevinger makes a clear distinction between conventionality and conformity in the discussion of this stage. A person characterized by conventional values may be at any position (above Symbiotic) on the model; while a Conformist represents the ego development of that one level and may even "conform" to comparatively nonconventional values of the group.

   Self-Aware Level: Transition from Conformist to Conscientious Stage. This level is the modal level for adults in American society. This stage on Loevinger's model corresponds to Kohlberg's Stage 4, which he also found to be the predominant stage of most societies (Kohlberg, 1972). Loevinger uses the term "level" to indicate that this phase is a transition from the Conformist to the Conscientious Stage. Even though it is theoretically transitional, research has indicated that it is a fairly stable position in adult life. This level represents a departure from the unexamined assumption of the Conformist Stage and a movement toward the complexity of reasoning required in the Conscientious Stage. Two salient characteristics of the individual at this level are increased self-awareness and an ability to appreciate multiple perspectives and alternatives. The individual becomes more *self* conscious and self processing and thus is able to move away from the external controls of the group. At the same time there is a new recognition of individual differences and the fact that multiple ways of thinking, feeling, and acting are possible.

   Conscientious Stage. The individual at this stage is characterized by having internalized rules and values and is able to see himself as an active choice maker and actor in the world. The complexity of reasoning evident at this stage allows the person both to generate for himself and appreciate in others a rich variety of emotions, perspectives, and contexts. A true capacity for empathy has developed as well as an internalized sense of responsibility for one's own actions and their consequences. The individual has developed the capacity for mutuality in his relationships with others and also aspires to a level of achievement consistent with his own standards. Thus the multiple facets of the ego (sense of self, conscious preoccupation, relationships with others, level of cognitive complexity) are becoming more integrated and autonomously directed.

   Individualistic Level: Transition from Conscientious to Autonomous Stages. Another transitional level, it primarily marks the person's heightened sense of individuality and an increased awareness of the emotional conflicts involved in the dependence/independence struggle. The individual becomes more tolerant of himself and others. At the Self-Aware Level he recognizes the existence of individual differences; at the Conscientious Stage he recognizes them in their complexity; now he is accepting them as truly legitimate, and will cherish, celebrate, and actively seek them at the Autonomous Stage. The individual at this level is more aware of the existence of inner conflict than before, has an increased ability to tolerate paradox and contradiction in life, is aware of the differences between process and outcome, and is more able to incorporate concepts such as psychological causality and development in thinking.

Autonomous Stage. Conceptual complexity is the most salient characteristic of this and the following stage. The individual sees reality as complex and multifaceted and is able to integrate apparently contradictory or incompatible ideas. He has a high tolerance for ambiguity and has a courageous capacity to confront and cope with the inner conflict that stems from conflicting needs, conflicting duties, and the conflicts between the two. The individual at this stage has an accurate awareness of his multiple roles and responsibilities and is interested in his own development and progress toward self-fulfillment. He allows autonomy in others and acknowledges his interdependence (Chickering, 1969, refers to the capacity for interdependence as the "capstone of autonomy") with others. He endorses and acts on broad, abstract social ideals such as fairness and justice.

Integrated Stage. This is the least described of the ten stages. Loevinger states that it is rare to find an individual functioning at this level. She suggests that the Integrated person has transcended the conflicts of the Autonomous Stage, has achieved an integrated sense of identity, and is best described in Maslow's concept of the Self-Actualized individual (Maslow, 1963).

instrumentation

Loevinger and Wessler (1970a) and associates have developed the Sentence Completion Test (SC) to measure position along their model of ego development. It is essentially a projective measure, consisting of thirty-six stems ("Being with other people . . ."; "My conscience bothers me if . . .") that are completed by the subject. Raters are trained to assign each response its appropriate ego level and to use an ogive rule scoring system to determine the subject's developmental stage category. Validity and reliability studies are on-going. Completed studies indicate that the SC is a reliable and valid measure of the construct of ego development, and that raters who have completed the self-training program outlined by Loevinger and Wessler (1970a) can achieve the rating accuracy levels of those who worked on the development of the SC itself. Loevinger and Wessler have provided a complete description of the model, the Sentence Completion Test, instructions for administering and scoring, and a rater training manual in their two-volume *Measuring Ego Development*. Although the (1970a, 1970b) manual contains four forms of the SC (one each for women and men, one each for girls and boys), and data that indicate no significant sex differences on studies of adolescent protocols, the rating cues and rules are all based on female responses, leaving the rater with the task of making appropriate adaptations for male protocols.

evaluation and implications of the model

Strengths

1. It is a model of human development that is not specific to age, race, socioeconomic status, or educational background. Given the changing nature of the college student population, it may prove to be a more adequate measure of development for today's pluralistic population than those models based on the traditional eighteen to twenty-two-year-olds.

2. It is a holistic model, reminding us of the interlocking nature of the multiple facets of the human personality. It serves as a reminder to the practitioner-educator that promotion of development in one area of a student's life is likely to affect other areas as well. The central concept of the unity of the personality stands in direct opposition to those who would view the student dichotomously—that his intellectual development is the exclusive domain of the faculty and his interpersonal development is the exclusive domain of student personnel. It might be thought of as integrating the psychosocial models with the cognitive developmental models and as providing stage descriptions along the Heath (1973) dimensions. From this perspective it appears to be the most comprehensive of the models presented in this sourcebook.

3. The model appears to be highly correlated with other major stage models. (See Table 1 for a formulation of the interrelationships.) Loevinger has said that the stage models depicted in the table appear to be "alternative formulations of what appear to me to be essentially the same concept" (1976, p. xi). In adapting this table from several of Loevinger's own, we have attempted to portray Heath's four critical domains of self, interpersonal relations, values, and intellect. These domains are, of course, similar to Loevinger's own. The reader is also directed to Loevinger's (1976, pp. 151-156) extensive discussion of the relationship between the ego development stages and Rogers' (1961) seven stage process of psychotherapy.

4. There exists a valid and reliable instrument to assess position on the model.

5. An extensive and effective manual for rater training has been published, making the use of the model much more likely.

Table 1. A Comparison of Loevinger Model with Other Major Stage Theorists

Loevinger — Approximate Ego Level	Loevinger — Interpersonal Style	Erikson — Developmental Tasks	Kohlberg — Basis of Moral Reasoning	Perry — Intellectual and Ethical Development
Presocial/Symbiotic	Symbiotic	Trust vs. Mistrust		
Impulsive	Receiving, dependent, exploitative		Stage 1 Fear of punishment by authority	Position 1 Dualism
Self-Protective	Wary, manipulative, exploitative	Autonomy vs. Shame and Doubt	Stage 2 Bargaining with authority to gain reward, avoid punishment	Position 2 Dualism
Conformist	Belonging, superficial niceness	Initiative vs. Guilt Industry vs. Inferiority	Stage 3 Seeking good relations and approval of family group	Position 3 Multiplicity prelegitimate
Self-Aware	Aware of self in relation to group; helping		Stage 4 Obedience to law and order in society	Position 4 Multiplicity
Conscientious	Intensive, responsible, mutual, concern for communication	Identity vs. Role Diffusion	Stage 5 Concern with individual rights and legal contract	Positions 5, 6 Relativism
Individualistic	Add: Dependence as emotional problem	Intimacy vs. Isolation	Stage 6 Concern with consistent, comprehensive ethical principles	
Autonomous	Add: Respect for autonomy; interdependence	Generality vs. Stagnation Ego Integrity vs. Despair		Positions 7, 8, 9
Integrated	Add: Cherishing of individuality			

Weaknesses

1. The model was built to assess developmental growth of women, and only later adapted for use with men. Yet it is purported to be universal and multicultural. The current rating manual uses examples taken exclusively from female protocols. Although some research has been conducted applying the model to men, much more needs to be done to satisfy the model's *human* development assumptions.

2. Although Loevinger consistently portrays ego development as the "master trait" that consists of multiple domains, the model is essentially a cognitive one. Currently we have no evidence that would allow us to know how much "weighting" the cognitive complexity factor has in comparison with the other primary factors discussed in the model. Loevinger resists such questions and asserts that such things cannot be measured with precision. The holism of the model is antithetical to a "sum of the parts" perspective, and thus Loevinger asserts that one cannot measure each of the domains separately and emerge with a total that equals the ego development of the person. Thus serious research questions are left unanswered by the assertion of holism.

3. Loevinger is not easily read or understood. We have found that her use of language and writing style may make her work less accessible to those who would otherwise be comfortable with her concepts. This may partially account for the paucity of studies using the model with college populations. Those studies that have been done have used ego development and Kohlberg (1972) stages as pre/post measures in deliberate psychological education efforts. Clearly studies of both a specific intervention and of a longitudinal nature need to be done in order to build a data base for college students.

4. Loevinger never addresses the prescriptive use of her theory. The practitioner must rely on already established prescriptive methods used with other stage models when beginning to use Loevinger's model. Of all the theorists we have studied, Loevinger remains the least explicit about the use of the model after assessment has taken place. She does not suggest what factors in the individual's environment are necessary to movement along the developmental continuum. In fact she asserts that deliberate attempts to facilitate development are misdirected.

references

Chickering, A. *Education and Identity.* San Francisco: Jossey-Bass, 1969.

Heath, R. "Form, Flow, and Full-Being Response to White's Paper." *The Counseling Psychologist,* 1973, *4,* 56–63.

Kohlberg, L. "A Cognitive-Developmental Approach to Moral Education." *Humanist,* 1972, *6,* 13–16.

Loevinger, J. "The Meaning and Measurement of Ego Development." *American Psychologist,* 1966, *21,* 195–206.

Loevinger, J. *Ego Development: Conceptions and Theories.* San Francisco: Jossey-Bass, 1976.

Loevinger, J., and Wessler, R. *Measuring Ego Development I: Construction and Use of a Sentence Completion Test.* San Francisco: Jossey-Bass, 1970a.

Loevinger, J., and Wessler, R. *Measuring Ego Development II: Scoring Manual for Women and Girls.* San Francisco: Jossey-Bass, 1970b.

Maslow, A. H. *Toward a Psychology of Being.* (2nd ed.) Princeton: Van Nostrand, 1963.

Rogers, C. R. *On Becoming a Person.* Boston: Houghton Mifflin, 1961.

*Ultimately student personnel workers are concerned
that students become mature and competent persons.
Heath's work offers a comprehensive view
of the development of the whole person.*

Douglas Heath's
model of maturing

carole widick
clyde a. parker
lee knefelkamp

As student personnel workers, we attempt to help students make career
decisions, manage the ins and outs of residence hall life, and cope with
various anxieties. Ultimately, we are concerned that our students
become mature and competent persons. In *Growing Up in College*,
Douglas Heath pointed to the central problem of our field arguing that
"the dilemma of the educator is that terms like growth, maturity, the
whole persona and human excellence are insufferably vague" (1968, p.
3), Heath has continually maintained that educational practice must
shift from a rhetorical to an empirical base. Stated simply, in order to
encourage maturity, we must have an objective understanding of the
factors which constitute it. Heath's work is an attempt to empirically
define maturity and describe the nature of maturing.

For the past twenty years, Heath has focused his efforts toward
the creation of a "Scientifically adequate and verifiable model of
maturing" (1977, p. 2). Heath's model is clearly a developmental
theory; however, he uses the term "maturing" rather than development as his central construct. This semantic difference reflects the

focus of his theory. In contrast to developmental approaches which identify age-specific tasks and decisions, Heath starts by delineating the processes (actually modes of psychological functioning) character-istic of the mature person. From that vantage point, his model charts the continuous movement from "immature" to "mature" ways of func-tioning.

Heath's work offers a comprehensive view of development. Most developmental theories are selective in focus, emphasizing a particular age range or a particular type of growth, such as moral development. Heath, however, takes the broad perspective, providing a conceptual scheme which includes and orders the many changes which occur as a person matures. His work therefore gives objective meaning to the development of the whole person.

Heath's model is abstract and complex particularly in its termi-nology. In order to present his work with clarity, we will first describe the model and then discuss it relative to college student development.

the model of maturing

From an extensive review of psychological theory and data, Heath conducted a logical factor analysis to derive his framework. The model, as he states (1977, p. 6), "is a classification map, a working set of categories which order the principal hypotheses which theorists claim distinguish mature from immature persons." The model of maturing specifies four self systems (or sectors of the individual) and five growth dimensions:

Self Systems	*Developmental Growth Dimensions*
Intellect	1. Becoming more able to represent experience symbolically
Values	2. Becoming allocentric or other-centered
Self-Concept	3. Becoming integrated
Interpersonal	4. Becoming stable
Relationships	5. Becoming autonomous

Heath suggests that maturation involves movement along the growth dimensions in each of the four areas of the self. For example, in maturing one becomes more allocentric in intellectual functioning, the establishment of values, in self-concept, and in relationships with others. In combining the growth dimensions and self systems, Heath emerges with a matrix (see Figure 1). The matrix provides twenty hypotheses or statements which define the realm of changes which occur during maturation.

The different self-systems or sectors are, for the most part, self-explanatory; however, the dimensions of development require description. The following section briefly discusses the meaning of the five dimensions without precisely relating each type of growth to each self

Figure 1. The Mature Personality

	Intellect	Values	Self-Concept	Interpersonal Relationships
Becoming able to symbolize experience	Able to evaluate one's own thought	Awareness of one's own beliefs	Awareness of self, accurate insights, self-analysis	Able to reflect about relationships, able to analyze why others act/ feel certain ways
Becoming allocentric (other-centered)	Thoughts are logical; tied to social reality	Centered around people, tolerant/ altruistic	Ability to see self as similar to others, empathy	Caring for others, ability to love, capacity for intimacy
Becoming progressively integrated	Able to problem-solve systematically, creative syntheses, coherence in thought	Workable world view, coherence in value commitments	Congruence of self-image; a realistic view of self	More openness, able to be wholly with another, capable of reciprocal, mutual, and cooperative relationships
Becoming stable (resistant to disruption by threat)	Thoughts stay organized; able to function consistently	Clear sustained commitment to set of values	Stable view of self; certainty certainty	Enduring friendships; commitment to specific other
Becoming autonomous	Use of data less imprisoned by bias	Independence of mind; integrity in belief and behavior	View of self as responsible; not overly reliant on others' perceptions	Relationships reflect autonomy, not sacrifice integrity for "belonging" non-manipulative

sector. To convey the comprehensive model, we have included a summary chart (Figure 1).

Increased Potential for Symbolization. Heath suggests that "to become mature is to develop the power to represent one's experiences as hunches, words, thought or other symbols" (1968, p. 6). In defining symbolization, he uses terms like "increased awareness," "a rich inner life," "heightened consciousness," "capacity to monitor one's own thought," and "accurate self and interpersonal insight." Thus, maturing involves increased cognitive capabilities that allow one to differentiate, examine, and articulate all elements of one's life.

A concrete example may clarify the contrast between different levels of symbolic maturity. If one were to ask a person to describe a friend, a less mature response might be "she's a good person. I think she's fun to be around." A more mature person might give a complex, almost metaphorical description of specific traits, such as "well, she's confident most of the time, but is uncertain about her ability to handle stress. She plays with ideas in remarkable ways; when I talk with her I'm always fascinated by the way she sees her own life in paradoxical terms. In fact, she seems to be a rather interesting cross between Don Quixote and Sancho Panza."

Becoming Allocentric. According to Heath, "a mature person is not as egocentric as an immature person nor is he as dominated by his own immediate needs. He is more socialized and other-centered. The process of maturing is a pervasively social process. . . . To become mature is to incorporate into oneself the social world into which one is being pushed and pulled" (1968, p. 8). The egocentrism of early childhood is described by the image of the "hiding" child who covers her eyes, concluding that since she cannot see, she cannot be seen. For the child, increasing allocentrism involves the discovery that others do not see precisely as she sees. In a basic sense, increasing allocentrism is that capacity to stand outside one's self and look at the world through other's eyes. In becoming allocentric, the person acquires a more complex and adequate picture of social reality.

Heath suggests that allocentric maturing is manifest in the following attitudes and skills: (1) an ability to look at problems from multiple perspectives; (2) increasing skill in socialized thought—thought that is precise and logical, thereby communicating effectively to others; (3) increased tolerance and adoption of humanistic values; (4) an increased ability to see oneself through others' eyes, thus expanding and becoming more objective in one's self-image; and (5) an increased ability to empathize with others, making possible more cooperative and caring relationships.

In describing a mature allocentrism, Heath provides a picture of the person whose intellectual perspective is similar to that of a social scientist and whose emotional stance reflects an ethical humanism. The allocentric person is able to be simultaneously objective and caring.

Becoming Integrated. For Heath, "maturing also means growing coherence and integration. Increasing differentiation and synthesis and greater complexity mark the mature person" (1977, p. 13). In essence, maturing involves the development of a more unified personality. Heath suggests that becoming more integrated can be seen in: (1) increased skills in analytic, relational, and synthetic thinking and systematic problem solving; (2) the development of a value system or world view; (3) increasing congruence between one's self-image and behavior; and (4) increasing ability to be more intimate and open in relationships.

Heath's discussion of integration in the self and interpersonal domain is remarkably similar to Carl Rogers' approach to self growth (Rogers, 1951). In maturing, a person becomes more aware and less defensive about the many sides of his or her personality. Strengths and weaknesses—the good and the not so good can be recognized, more-over, these seeming disparities are incorporated into a viable identity. The private self-image is congruent with social behavior. This inte-grated self-image is then reflected in integrative relationships, "a maturing person who knows and accepts what he is, can open himself to his friends, not holding back, hiding, or defending himself in his intimate relationships" (Heath, 1968, p. 13).

Becoming Stable. Heath introduces the stability dimension with the following definition, "To say that a person becomes more stable is to say that his intellectual skills, values, image of himself, and interper-sonal relations become more resistant to threat" (1968, p. 13). Increas-ing stability is manifest in these skills and behavior patterns: (1) increased capacity to think effectively under pressure; (2) more consistently held values; (3) less fluctuation in one's self-image; and (4) increasing ability to make stable and enduring commitments to other people.

Increased stability involves acquiring perceptions and skills which make stress and environmental change less disorganizing. As almost any student services worker can attest, transition into college is often a disruptive experience; within a month many eighteen-year-old freshmen complain that they cannot concentrate and do not know who they are or what they believe. In contrast, many older returning stu-dents are ultimately less disrupted although they also suffer from initial confusion and anxiety; their personalities and commitments are often more mature, and the college experience while challenging, does not provoke large-scale personality disorganization.

Becoming Autonomous. Heath suggests that a "maturing person becomes less manipulable by his environment and less driven by infantile wishes and conflict. . . . This is not to imply that there are no identifiable determinants of a mature person's decisions; rather the locus of the decisions has been moved from both the environment and his past history into his own contemporary self-structure" (1968, p. 15). Becoming autonomous is manifest in: (1) increasing ability to make intellectual judgments without being unduly influenced by personal biases; (2) an increasing ability to behave in accord with one's principles even when challenged or threatened by others; (3) the ability to sustain one's self-image and selectively consider other's opinions; and (4) the establishment of relationships which make room for differing needs and separate loyalties

In behavioral terms, increased autonomy would manifest itself in a variety of ways. The mature person would probably be both less conforming and less adamantly independent. Ideals or personal style would not be altered radically simply to maintain a relationship nor would absolute credence be granted to others' evaluations of him or her.

Figure 1 abstracts the traits typical of maturity. A cautionary note: The chart is not intended to outline a set of developmental end points. Heath conceives of development as an unending journey. Whatever the individual's state, continual adaptation to new demands and more complex environments will refine the capacity to symbolize, tune into social realities, integrate, stabilize, and become more autonomous in the different self systems.

For Heath, development is essentially an adaptive process. He views the person as a developing system characterized by an internal equilibrium. If the individual is somehow disorganized, a self-regulating principle operates, leading the person to try new responses in an effort to reestablish internal balance. If conditions are right, the new responses encourage maturing changes; if not, the person may cope with the disorganization by regressing to immature ways of behaving.

Heath postulates a basic cycle of adaptive responses which follow disorganization. He argues that the cycle of adaptations brings about particular sequential maturing changes. The following diagram outlines the adaptive cycle:

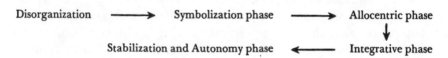

A concrete example may clarify this cycle and the types of maturing which it creates. Suppose an individual fresh out of graduate school begins working in a large state university on the student services staff. He comes in with a fairly coherent view of himself and his professional role. Within a few weeks, he has found to his dismay that he is not too effective. He is surprised that some of his ideas do not work; even worse, sometimes they are regarded as naive or unrealistic. He begins to feel less competent and questions his professional commitment. *Disorganization* has set in. He starts the adaptation cycle trying to *symbolize* what is happening. In this case he may focus upon his self-concept and professional values. He tries to conceptualize what he experiences — what am I doing wrong? Are "they" so unaware of new developments in the field that I cannot communicate with them? Is my timing wrong? Am I really committed to helping students? The *allocentric phase* involves a turning to others or alternative perspectives. The young professional begins to talk with other staff to see how they view him and the field. He may read a few books about the realities of higher education. He finds himself drawn to conference sessions that focus on the new staff member. Out of this allocentric search, he begins to formulate a more complex perception of himself, his professional values, and the field. He moves into the *integrative phase,* trying to create a coherent new approach. As an example, he may stay committed to the idea of helping students yet realize the necessity of a disciplinary role. He may find a way to differentiate his view of helping students in which discipline can be seen as a legitimate way of helping. Finally the new approach begins to work and he becomes more *stable and autonomous* as a functioning professional. This cycle would create many different types of maturing, particularly in the self-concept. In a more general sense, this cycle of adaptations describes the sequence of changes which occur in young adult maturing.

For Heath, development involves an intrinsic directionality; we tend to move along the five dimensions toward more mature functioning. His view, however, is interactive: The environment may facilitate or inhibit that maturing. There appears to be two important roles played by the environment in the developmental process. First, it may or may not provoke the necessary disorganization which gives impetus to growth. Second, it may or may not provide supports which help the person mature. Heath argues that disorganization can lead in two directions: regression or developmental progression. Thus, the environment needs to provide help, making it possible for the person to reflect, gain new perspectives, and create coherent ways of thinking about the self, values, and relationships.

research

Heath has undertaken a number of research projects to test the validity of his model. One major study involved a longitudinal investigation of student development at Haverford College. His purposes in this study were: (1) to describe the patterns of maturing that occurred during and following college years, and (2) to identify major determinants of those maturing changes.

Method of Study. Heath employed a systematic case study approach in his Haverford investigation. Randomly selected student groups were studied in their freshman and senior years.

As previously noted, the dimensions of maturing are defined globally in terms of general orientations, perceptions, and interactive styles. To assess growth along the five dimensions, Heath used a range of different types of measures to operationalize his constructs.

Standardized personality and interest measures (for example, the MMPI, Allport-Vernon-Lindsey Study of Values, Strong Vocational Interest Blank) were used to ascertain maturing on specific dimensions. Heath used particular scales that seemed logically related to certain domains of the maturity scheme; for example, the Repression score (MMPI) was identified as a measure of self-awareness (symbolization).

Two tests were also constructed to directly test the maturity model: the Self-Image Questionnaire (SIQ) and the Perceived Self Questionnaire (PSQ). The SIQ asks the person to rate his or her traits on thirty bipolar scales; this test provides a way to measure maturity of self-concept. The PSQ, a fifty-item questionnaire, assesses maturity on each of the dimensions for each of the self sectors. Heath provides evidence suggesting these two tests are reliable and valid measures of the scheme (1968, p. 82).

In addition to objective measures, Heath used an interview format to assess student perceptions. The interviews were rated to provide student self-assessment of changes in personality during college and environmental determinants which brought about such change.

Space does not permit an extended evaluation of the measures in Heath's research strategy. For that information, the reader is referred to *Growing Up in College* (Heath, 1968). Suffice it to say, Heath's approach was empirically rigorous, emphasized content validity, and used convergent measures to operationalize and test the model.

Findings. To convey the nature of maturing for Haverford men, we will list Heath's major findings and present his interpretation of the data (1968, pp. 116–174):

1. Seniors appear to be more mature than freshmen and more mature than they were as freshmen.

2. Seniors report more maturing than freshmen.

3. The rate of maturing varies in different sectors, but the pattern conforms to the theory of maturing.

4. The pattern of growth was consistent for most students. Major changes were initiated during the first half of the freshman year. These changes occurred as the result of the disorganizing influence of

the college. The remaining years of college appeared to be a working through of that initial change.

5. Overextended development in one area resulted in turning to other self areas. Haverford students tended to be overly intellectual; the confrontation with other students appeared to redirect their concerns to their interpersonal development.

6. The major and most significant maturing effects as perceived by students were increasing integration of intellectual skills (critical thinking skills), increasing symbolization of self (self-awareness), and increasing integration of interpersonal relationships (ability to be close and open with others).

7. Maturing was not and probably cannot be completed during college years. Some of the impacts of college are not recognized until viewed from a postcollege vantage point. In follow-up studies, Haverford alumni reported that college helped them attain stable values which combined with postcollege experiences and fostered an integrated and stable identity.

This brief recital of major findings indicates the types of maturing that appear to occur in college. In *Growing Up in College*, Heath presents an extensive discussion of specific results which we will not attempt to review here. Heath (1968, p. 176) interprets his findings in the following way:

> Is there an orderly sequential development to the maturing process in young adults? Our hunch is that there may be, and that it is initiated by induced instability, to which the person responds with increased awareness, and more allocentric and integrative adaptive attempts. Eventually an adaptive solution is evolved that stabilizes and begins to function more autonomously. This sequence occurs at different rates in different sectors of the personality. The developmental process is completed first in the maturation of intellective-cognitive skills, next in the same sex and then opposite sex personal relationships. The maturing of a person's values tends to follow the stabilization of his personal relationships. The maturing of the self-concept takes longer and goes through more transitional stages, eventuating in a stable integration with the person's values.

College students appeared to mature most along the symbolization, allocentric, and integrative dimensions: They became more aware of others, themselves, and their values. They were able to think more logically and were more able to view themselves and others with both objectivity and empathy. They developed skills that allowed them to think in an integrative fashion and relate to others in more intimate ways. By graduation, most students were beginning to fashion an integrated value system. However, in several areas students seemed to make limited progress. As Heath states (1968, p. 175), the senior's "unfulfilled developmental tasks upon graduation are stabilization of heterosexual relationships, the integration and eventual stabilization of his values and self-concept, and the development of increased autonomy." We might say that the college experience left the student ready for the adult world but unfinished in his growth. The development of a stable, autonomous identity and value system seems to require the tests provided by job experiences, marriage, and other long-term decisions.

Heath identified a number of elements in the college environment that contribute to such maturing. In basic agreement with other observers of the college scene (Chickering, 1969; Perry, 1970), he suggested that the principal sources of impact were interpersonal (roommates, close same-sex friends) and intellectual and academic determinants (the ethos of the college, courses which explicitly focused on values, faculty who were models of maturity, and an honor system).

Convergent Research. Placing Heath's model and findings in the broader context of developmental research, a substantial body of parallel evidence can be found. Though cognitive developmental theorists assume stages of development, their descriptions of stages typical of young adulthood closely relate to Heath's findings. Perry's (1970) description of intellectual development can be seen as charting the shift to more symbolic, allocentric (multiplicity stage), and integrative (relativism stage) thought. Kohlberg's work (1969) generally confirms the changes in the value sector while Loevinger's ego model delineates similar shifts in self-concept and interpersonal orientations (see Loevinger, 1976; Loevinger, Wessler, and Redmore, 1970).

Perhaps the most interesting convergent line of research is that of Arthur Chickering (1969). The two models construct the developmental universe in different ways; Chickering talks of dimensions but appears to focus on age-specific tasks, whereas Heath delineates continuous dimensions. A brief paralleling of the two models conveys a definite similarity in some of their constructs:

Heath	*Chickering*
Symbolization of interpersonal relationships	Social competence
Allocentric values	Humanizing of values
Allocentric relationships	Tolerance of others
Integration of self-concept	Establishing identity
Integration of values	Personalizing of values

While Heath and Chickering present remarkably similar conclusions about young adult growth, one major and significant difference is evident. Heath's study suggests that the development of stable and autonomous values, relationships, and self-concept typically occur in postcollege years; Chickering's model gives more credence to those changes occurring in the college context. Heath's data tend to be supported by studies of adulthood (Levinson and others, 1978) and our personal observations; however further empirical study is required to clarify this issue.

a critique of the maturity model

Douglas Heath presents a model of maturity which has been systematically studied and validated in longitudinal and cross-cultural research. The model is one of the few attempts to provide a comprehensive view of development. His scheme of maturing is systematic, complex, and at times, different in terminology. If one examines the matrix (Figure 1), a picture of specific attitudinal and behavior changes is evident. However, the sheer magnitude of these factors is a bit overwhelming; it is difficult to think with Heath's constructs. The comprehensive nature of his work, a theoretical strength, is difficult to translate into the practitioner's frame of reference.

The major limitation of Heath's scheme rests with his delineation of the process of developmental change. His discussion is abstract and global in focus. He suggests that disorganization leads to a cycle of adaptive maturing responses. However, the adaptive cycle is descriptive rather than explanatory. For example, Heath suggests that disorganization provokes symbolization, the person tries to make sense of the experience. But efforts to symbolize may not necessarily lead to increased skill in symbolizing. Heath does not explain the factors which actually cause those skills to develop. Basically, a more precise explanation of the psychological processes which underlie the adaptive cycle is needed.

If we focus on the disorganization/adaptation cycle, Heath's descriptions provide only a general rendering of the change process. As practitioners, we need to know more specifically what constitutes disorganization. It is particularly important to note that Heath disavows stage development (Heath, 1978). While Erikson (1963) places great importance on crises as essential considerations in development, Heath uses the milder term disorganization. For example, Heath's self systems are supposed to develop systematically toward greater maturity on the dimensions described above as the adaptive cycle repeats. By contrast, for Erikson each stage focuses at a particular crisis. Specifically, for college students, the identity crisis. Thus, these two theorists offer alternative hypotheses. One describes a gradual accommodation and adaptation of the self system to the influence of the environment; the other development is marked by crisis of polar choice, for example, identity versus identity diffusion. The importance of these two different constructs of development cannot be overemphasized.

Heath asserts the need for environmental supports which help the student adapt and hence develop. For Haverford students, he suggests that the ethos of the college and peer relationships played a facilitative role. However, Heath does not provide a functional definition of supports. One cannot discern what actually aids symbolizing or integrating. Although he discusses environmental determinants, Heath does not functionally link environmental components to specific growth process. Thus an individual working in a different type of college would have difficulty using Heath's framework to identify possible supports peculiar to that institution.

Heath's research findings reflect the maturing of male students in a distinctive institution. We should be cautious in generalizing from Haverford students to other students in different institutions. Although the general direction and cycle of growth may be generic, the degree of actual maturing may vary widely. The model, like all theoretical frameworks, requires investigation with different student populations.

Regardless of certain limitations, Heath's model is a substantial contribution. He provides a scheme which outlines development comprehensively. He enables us to more adequately define the meaning of student development in global terms.

implications

Heath's model and substantiating research provide a vantage point for considering the meaning of student development and student personnel practice. From our perspective, Heath's work does not give specific guidance for day-to-day practice. The model is a grand design and can best be used to help us consider the outcomes of an ideal educational experience. Heath's model can help us to articulate developmental goals and focus our efforts. The maturity model is the only framework which defines student development comprehensively. Heath outlines the domain specifying the range of possible goals that could be addressed in a developmental approach to practice. His work helps us realize that we must consider intellect as well as identity, value questions as well as relationships.

Most important, Heath's writings serve to illuminate the essential interconnections between intellectual and social development. In fact, a maturing of intellect seems to be a necessary condition for self-growth. Heath's model clarifies the nature of intellectual development, allowing us to see maturing as the acquisition of skills which can be viewed apart from the academic context. The student personnel field has often been subject to a conflict over its functions: We sometimes assume students' intellects are the province of the faculty, while their social-emotional growth belongs to the student personnel worker. This is an artificial and limiting dichotomy. Students cannot be divided into separate intellectual and social selves; student personnel practice cannot address the social and ignore the intellectual domain. Students do not make career decisions, struggle to become more tolerant of others, or break away from parents without thinking in some fashion. In helping students manage social decisions and tasks, we need to pay attention to their intellectual development. By partially shifting our focus from helping students choose a career or get along with roommates to helping them think about choosing a career or better conceptualize interpersonal relationships, we may more readily address their developmental needs. Heath's model presents a picture of the whole student and directs our attention to a broader definition of practice.

references

Chickering, A. *Education and Identity*. San Francisco: Jossey-Bass, 1969.

Erikson, E. *Childhood and Society* (2nd Ed.). New York: W. W. Norton and Co., 1963.

Heath, D. *Growing Up in College*. San Francisco: Jossey-Bass, 1968.

Heath, D. *Maturity and Competence: A Transcultural View*. New York: Gardner Press, 1977.

Heath, D. "A Model of Becoming a Liberally Educated and Mature Student." In C. Parker (Ed.), *Encouraging Development in College Students*. Minneapolis: University of Minnesota Press, 1978.

Kohlberg, L. "Stage and Sequence: The Cognitive Developmental Approach to Socialization." In D. Goslin (Ed.), *Handbook of Socialization Theory and Research*. New York: Rand McNally, 1969.

Levinson, D., and others. *The Season's of a Man's Life*. New York: Alfred A. Knopf, 1978.

Loevinger, J. *Ego Development: Conceptions and Theories*. San Francisco: Jossey-Bass, 1976.

Loevinger, J., Wessler, R., and Redmore, C. *Measuring Ego Development: Construction and Use of a Sentence Completion Test*. Vol. 1. San Francisco: Jossey-Bass, 1970.

Loevinger, J., Wessler, R., and Redmore, C. *Measuring Ego Development: Scoring Manual for Women and Girls*. Vol. 2. San Francisco: Jossey-Bass, 1970.

Perry, W., Jr. *Forms of Intellectual and Ethical Development in the College Years*. New York: Holt, Rinehart and Winston, 1970.

Rogers, C. *Client-Centered Therapy*. New York: Houghton Mifflin, 1951.

*Heath suggests that different types of students respond
to different sources of support and different
challenges for growth. His model provides important
information for the practitioner who has the
responsibility to design programs which
deliberately encourage development.*

Roy Heath's model of personality typologies

lee knefelkamp
clyde a. parker
carole widick

The work of Roy Heath (1964, 1973) serves both as a reminder of the
importance of individual differences and as a descriptive model of how
those differences can affect an individual's movement toward maturity. The apparent simplicity of the model (three types of personalities
capable of movement toward an idealized description of maturity) is
deceptive. Heath's model, like all others, is a product of the assumptions, experiences, observations, and synthesis of its creator. Heath is a
clinical psychologist, a professor of psychology, an academic advisor,
and an individual who was educated and continues to work in Ivy
League colleges and universities. The model is based on his own intensive case studies of thirty-six Princeton male undergraduates as they
progressed through their four years in college in the early 1950s. As
such, it is one of the best examples of the case study method and the
usefulness of its findings.

The model is based on the interfacing of two dimensions. The
first dimension is that of "ego functioning" or maturity level of the
individual, "the manner in which the self interacts with the world,

achieves its satisfaction, and defends itself from threats to its survival" (Heath, 1973, p. 59). The individual moves through a series of three developmental maturity levels (low, medium, high) on the way to achieving an idealized level of maturity referred to as a "Reasonable Adventurer." The second dimension is that of individual style or type, the person's basic temperamental approach to life. Three personality types are based on the manner in which the individual regulates the "dynamic tension" between the inner, instinctual, feeling self and the outer, more rational self. Each type proceeds toward maturity in an individualistic manner, and each may achieve the maturity level of the Reasonable Adventurer. The model integrates developmental (maturity) level with temperamental style (personality type) presenting a holistic picture of the self.

maturity level

Maturity level is similar to the stage concept discussed in previous chapters; development proceeds along a sequential and hierarchical continuum. Each of the three levels represents qualitatively different levels of ego functioning. Individuals at each level differ in the ways they regulate their behaviors, feelings, thought processes, and actions. In his later work Heath (1973) referred to this dimension as "Form" and to the three levels as poor, fair, and good form. Regardless of personality type, individuals at each of the levels have characteristics in common. Low level ego functioning individuals are characterized by a lack of awareness about themselves and others; they are more restricted and narrow in their thinking, more afraid to take risks, and more defensive and anxious when they feel the self threatened; they also tend to be externally controlled. Individuals at the medium level are becoming more aware and accepting of themselves and others, more able to cope with diversity, more integrated and coherent in their thoughts, feelings, and behaviors, and more competent in the way they achieve the tasks in their lives. Individuals at the higher level are characterized by a high degree of integration in ego functioning; they have become genuinely accepting of self and others; they appreciate and seek individual differences; their world is more diverse and more complex; and they have begun to achieve a stable sense of competence about the manner in which they carry out their life tasks. The model assumes Erikson's (1968) epigenetic principle: each of the levels is built on the strengths and achievements of those that have come before and each contains a preview of and is an enabler of the levels that will follow. An individual cannot skip a level in the model, although individuals do proceed at varying rates.

One of the major contributions of Heath's model is its attention to the importance of individual differences. His work calls our attention to this vital aspect of the students with whom we work. But he also remains mindful of our commonalities, our characteristics shared with others and the fact that those shared characteristics can be used to place us in meaningful group classifications, such as "types." In her review of typology models, Tyler (1978) says that the oldest way of organizing knowledge about people is to classify them into types. Heath defined the types in his model according to the "kinds of personality patterns that [the individuals] may manifest" (1973, p. 58). Loevinger (1977) has stated that this "patterning of activity is the most individual thing about a person" (p. 107). Heath's three types are not defined by a collection of content interests or traits, as is true of most typologies, but by temperamental differences which lead to different "patterns" in the ways individuals regulate impulses.

Heath relies on psychoanalytic theory when he defines the source of these different patterns as the "dynamic tension" between the inner self world and the outer self world. Each individual utilizes an underlying "consciousness filter" system to regulate the tension between the two worlds. The three primary personality types each have a distinctly different pattern of impulse control resulting from a different filter system. The placement of the three primary types along a temperamental continuum is determined by the degree to which the consciousness filter system allows the instinctual and the rational worlds of the self to be aware of and interact with one another. "There are differences between persons in the functional limits of the filter capacity range. . . . I suspect that the limits of one's filter capacity is a reflection of what is generally called one's temperament or inherent disposition" (1973, p. 58).

The three types and their locations (from left to right) along the continuum are: Type X — Constricted Filter Capacity, Type Y — Semi-Constricted, and Type Z — Porous Filter. The types are characterized by differing defense systems, dispositions toward the motive behind social involvement (to belong for the X, to be esteemed for the Y, to be noticed for the Z), sources of reward and punishment, environments that challenge or support; by their attitude towards self; by the manner in which they tend to interact with both people and environments; and by the very tasks that they find either appealing or frightening.

Although Heath discusses only three primary types, his use of a continuum reminds us that individuals could be placed anywhere along the temperamental line depending on the degree of constrictedness or porosity of their filter systems. We have attempted to convey this by the three "range" lines in Figure 1 representing the overlap of each of the primary types from the most constricted X to the most porous Z. Heath was able to place each of the 36 students in his original study on the model not only by level of maturity (the vertical axis), but also by the degree of porosity of his filter system (the horizontal axis). This "fine-tuning" of type and maturity level raises the possibility of an individual having combinations of type Y with types X and Z, but his theory disallows the possibility of type X and Z combinations unless they occur at the upper levels of maturity on the developmental axis.

Individuals manifest the most pronounced differences across typologies at the lowest maturity level, hence the lower they are on the developmental dimension, the easier it is to discriminate between types. As a person becomes more mature, he will exhibit less of the stereotyped characteristics of his type and more of the mature forms of his stylistic approach to the world. Types maintain their individualistic qualities and do not merge into one "super-type." The Reasonable Adventurer reflects the stylistic variations of each of the types, but those variations are less pronounced than at the lower developmental levels as a result of the maturing process.

the three primary types

Type X. Type X has difficulty responding to his inner self and being aware of his inner feelings. At the lowest level of ego functioning an individual's emotional self is unconsciously "embedded" deep within him, resulting in an unawareness of who he is and how he really feels. This lack of knowledge about self produces the following characteristics: (1) a need to avoid entanglements and commitments by maintaining a neutral position or stance; (2) a tendency to be a passive participant in relationships and in the academic world; (3) a tendency to depend on an authority figure for answers and solutions to dilemmas; (4) a need to deny negative thoughts and feelings and to see only the positive aspects of a situation; (5) a fear of risk taking and change; and (6) a strong need "to belong" and to help relationships be harmonious and not ridden with conflict.

The *medial X* has begun to be more aware of self and has begun to learn how to cope with the presence of conflict in relationships and diversity of opinions in the academic, social, and work worlds. While his first impulse is to seek the opinions of others or to avoid taking a stand, he is learning to think and act more independently. He will remain in the peacemaker or maintenance role in a group, but growing in confidence in his ability to confront or to disagree. The medial X is getting in touch with both positive and negative feelings

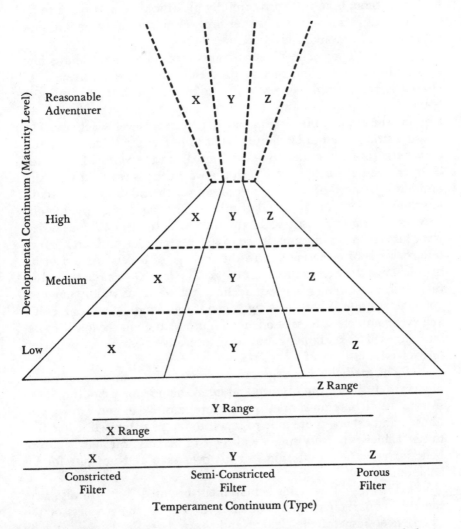

Figure 1. Model of Heath's Reasonable Adventurer

and is just beginning to accept the legitimacy of existence of those feelings.

The *high level* X has developed a more aware and integrated self. He not only recognizes the array of his feelings, but has accepted them as a legitimate part of who he is. While still most comfortable when finding structure and guidance from an authority figure, he has begun to use his own structure and is capable of independent thought and action. His motive behind being a peacemaker is now to facilitate the accomplishment of tasks as well as to maintain peace. Conflict remains stress producing, but it is no longer viewed as always negative and always to be avoided. The high X has begun to develop both the skills and the courage to initiate and to lead as well as to receive and to follow—although he will very carefully pick the time and place to do so. His skills as a watcher/observer are well honed and they are now beginning to be strategically directed.

The Y Type. The Y's semi-constricted filter system allows him to be more aware of his feeling state than the more constricted X. However, this partial awareness results in the Y's distrust (and even fear) of those impulses and the active, conscious effort to avoid confronting the impulse life by engaging in an intense level of activity. The X has a strong need to facilitate and keep peace; the Y has an inordinate need to achieve and to assert himself on the world. Frequently characterized as being at war with the world, he is really at war with himself, convinced of his own lack of self worth and desperately wanting the affection and approval of others. The *low Y* is a "pseudoself" striving to be a composite of all the successful things he thinks others want him to be. In his impatience to succeed and his profound fear of failure, he is often insensitive to the feelings of others. Afraid of his own feelings, he denies them in others. The low Y is characterized by dichotomies: thinking is good, feeling is a waste of time; change is good, status-quo is bad; leading is good, following is bad; one either achieves complete success or one is a failure. Although the low Y represents himself as a thinking, rational, objective person, he is not an introspective or insightful one.

The *medial Y* has begun to experience the legitimacy of points of view that differ from his own and hence he no longer holds quite so firm to his dichotomous rules. He is more sensitive to and forgiving of himself and others, more able to relax, to laugh at himself, to be free to not achieve in every single endeavor of activity. He has begun to believe that others value him for his own sake and not just for his achievements.

The *high Y* remains achievement oriented, but will also take the risk of participating in activities for fun or the newness of the experience. Some of the rigidity and sharp defensive edges are gone and hence the high Y can more effectively express emotions and empathize with the emotions of others. While he still prefers the thinking mode, feeling has become legitimate. He no longer insists that his rules should be for everyone, because others have become legitimate.

The Z Type. The Z's filter system is the most porous, and the Z is often characterized by impulsivity and variability of mood. The *low Z* is aware of his impulses and feeling states but is neither insightful about nor in control of them. He is at their mercy. As such he often has difficulty completing tasks because his attention will be captured by something new or he becomes bored and lacks the self-discipline to continue. While the low Y is orderly to the point of rigidity, the Z is a free spirit who will foil any and all attempts at scheduling and structuring. The low Z often has communication difficulties because he often cannot make himself understood as the jumble of ideas, thoughts, and feelings that he has come pouring out in a seemingly unconnected manner. It is almost as if he trips over himself in his efforts to get everything said. The low Z's academic and interpersonal effort are sporadic, confusing to himself as well as his teachers and friends. The low Z alternates between feeling lonely and misunderstood and feeling unique, original, creative, and capable of anything and everything.

The *medial Z* has begun to learn how to control and regulate his impulses so that he is a more consistent performer in social and academic realms. He is more able to express his inner feelings in a manner others can understand and respond to. Still subject to wide variations of mood, he is more aware of what will trigger them and how he can behave so that he is more in control.

The *high Z* has learned to direct his creativity in ways that will promote the completion of a project and to provide the structure that will enable others to more easily understand him. He has also learned to protect himself from those who are not attuned to his open sensitivity and vulnerability. And he has discovered the consistent aspects of his personality which serve as the core around which his idiosyncratic characteristics revolve.

the reasonable adventurer

The *Reasonable Adventurer* is Heath's term for an individual who has reached the level of mature, integrated ego functioning. The Reasonable Adventurer is characterized by six attributes: intellectuality, close friendships, independence in value judgments, tolerance of ambiguity, breadth of interest, and sense of humor. The Reasonable Adventurer is an individual who has integrated his instinctual and rational self and has a confident sense of being able to act in the world. He possesses a wide array of behaviors and skills and is able to react appropriately to almost any situation. He is reasonable, thoughtful, and accepting of others and their different perspectives and values. He communicates well and is able to be both independent and interdependent in action and decision making. He is characterized by an ability to find or develop ways to satisfy himself. A personal resourcefulness enables him to look forward with confidence to a future of exciting possibilities.

Although highly integrated, the Reasonable Adventurer is also highly individualistic and does not conform to any one behavioral model. Stylistic characteristics remain. For example:

- A Reasonable Adventurer who is an X type would still wish to serve a maintenance role in a group and to be a more passive than active participant, but the mature expression of this characteristic could be the behind the scenes organizing of a conference in which he brings many diverse people together to explore, discuss, and debate a common theme.
- A Reasonable Adventurer who is a Y type would still have a drive for achievement and getting things done, but could channel that energy into providing leadership and encouragement to a group of individuals who shared a commitment to the process or the end goal.
- A Reasonable Adventurer who is a Z would likely still respond to unexpected flights of fancy or whimsy, but would be able to harness that creative energy to produce innovative programs or curricula that would affect students positively.

It is important to remember that being a Reasonable Adventurer is not an end point. Rather it is having achieved a perspective on and a mature way of functioning in the world that enables one to continue to explore and experience, as Murray in the movie, *1,000 Clowns*, would say, "all the marvelous possibilities."

assessment techniques

The Original Study. Heath's clinical judgment was the assessment used in his original study. A student's place in the model was determined by the intersection of his position on the developmental and the temperamental dimensions. A student's position on the developmental continuum was determined by his score on three psychological scales that Heath developed:

Scale I   Satisfaction from academic work
Scale II   Satisfaction from friendship with peers
Scale III Self-understanding and acceptance

Each scale had five maturity levels ranging one (low) to five (high). Thus a student's scores could range from three to fifteen total points. Heath himself made the judgments as to the number of points each student would receive from information gained in interviews and his own clinical appraisal of their maturity level. He does not provide us with the exact score cut-offs for being considered at a high, medium, or low level of maturity. Heath also used the interview transcripts to determine the students' position along the temperamental dimension. Detailed examples of this process are provided in Appendix A of *The Reasonable Adventurer*.

The Modes of Existence Test. In the 1970s Heath began to work on a more standardized format for assessing position on the model.

The Modes of Existence Test (1976b) consists of eleven different "modes," or descriptions of types of people, each one-half a page in length. Nine of the modes are indicative of the nine positions in Heath's model (three levels of maturity for each of the three types). There are two additional modes: one is a disclaimer for those who dislike the test, and one represents a hypothetical type on which Heath is collecting data.

Students are asked to read all of the type descriptors and to select and rank on a Likert scale the two or three modes that most resemble themselves and to indicate the mode that least resembles themselves. Students are also encouraged to change or modify words and phrases in order to make the modes more accurately reflect their own self portrait. These changes affect the scorer's interpretation of the students' type.

With the exception of a recent study done at the University of Maryland (Agar, 1978), we know of no research that reports reliability or validity studies on the Modes of Existence Test. Agar (1978) undertook a two part research project at the University of Maryland to assess the validity of the Modes of Existence Test and of a behaviorally oriented instrument to assess Heath's position on the selection of resident hall advisors. The sample consisted of 45 undergraduates who were employed as Resident Advisors by the Office of Resident Life. All subjects were administered the Modes of Existence Test and the Resident Advisor Heath Typology Instrument developed by Agar. A group of three expert raters were asked to independently assign typology classifications to each of the 45 RA's whom they knew well enough to classify confidently. Procedures were used to determine a consensus rating for each student and a level of confidence for each rating. Utilizing predetermined decision rules for scoring the Modes of Existence Test, typology classifications were obtained for each of the students. The correlation between the Expert Consensus typing and the Modes of Existence typing was +.75. It should be noted that the correlations were for type classification only and not for the student's position on the developmental continuum. No data have been collected to determine the accuracy of the instrument with respect to developmental level. Although encouraging, the results of the Agar study are based on a relatively small and comparatively homogeneous sample of student leaders and on logical, but untested, scoring rules for determining typology from the student's responses to the instrument. Clearly much work needs to be done in the areas of validity and reliability testing and in the creation of uniform scoring rules before the practitioner can use the model to assess an individual's position in a confident and heuristic manner.

critique of the model

Strengths

1. The major contribution of this framework is that it incorporated two dimensions necessary to making sense of the college experience. It is important that we recognize student differences which persist even through the highest levels of development. Heath highlights a set of student types which may be of use to us in planning college environments.
2. Heath's work is centered in higher education. His framework thus needs no translation to make sense for college age individuals.
3. Heath writes in plain, understandable language.
4. This framework is holistic. The student is seen as an intellectual and social being simultaneously. For Heath, development is toward integration of aspects of the self and he identifies the interrelatedness of intellectual demands and interpersonal commitments.
5. The practitioner can use the model with both student and staff populations to assess job descriptions and tasks.

Limitations

1. Heath's framework is inadequately spelled out. No clear description is given of what causes movement through the steps or stages of development.
2. The clinical approach does not lend itself to easy use of the model. No validated method of type and developmental level diagnosis is available at present, although Heath has developed an assessment measure called the Modes of Existence Test (1976b) and Agar (1978) has developed an instrument to assess Heath typology and job functions for resident hall peer advisors.
3. Minimal research has been carried out using the scheme after the study at Princeton. Research needs to be done to determine whether or not the model is applicable to women as well as men and is still appropriate for the college population two decades after its original formulation.
4. We do not now know the relationship (if any) of Heath's developmental dimension with cognitive stage theory or how his model of ego development relates to the ego development models of other theorists.

implications for practitioners

Heath suggests that different types of students respond to different sources of support and different challenges for growth. His model provides important information for the practitioner who has the responsibility to design programs which deliberately encourage development. A series of specific questions are appropriate for each type: (1) What are the sources of support for this type? (2) What are the sources of challenge? and (3) What are relevant content areas based on the most difficult developmental tasks for each type? We will illustrate with three case study examples.

Type Y Leaders. Student leaders on campus are often Y types. Heath's theory appears validated in our practical experience and in our analysis of these students. These leaders are often talented but prone to try to do too much and thus not do all things very well. They are often confident—even arrogant—publicly, but prone to enormous self-doubt in private; are genuinely concerned about programs that would benefit others, but frequently are seen as insensitive and power hungry by their peers. To be effective, these students need to stop and look at themselves in a more introspective and insightful manner; they need to feel cared for and esteemed; and they need to develop empathic skills. The Leadership Development Program in the Office of Campus Activities at the University of Maryland includes an academic course in group dynamics and leadership designed and taught specifically for campus leaders. The course process and content encourage the students to examine themselves and their leadership styles in an in-depth manner through their study of leadership models and styles, student typology models, analysis of their needs and how their needs are met, and through a specific confrontation of the impact of their leadership as it enables or hinders others in the maturing process. The course is highly regarded by students who participate and is an example of how theory and practice can work together to promote the maturity of college students.

Ignored Type X. Students who are X types often have highly developed group facilitation skills, yet their tendency to remain quietly in the background has often resulted in their not being selected for leadership or peer advising roles. The staff of the Orientation Office at the University of Maryland was concerned that they might not select leaders who would help the group maintain itself throughout the long training and summer orientation sessions but who would likely produce in highly competent ways if given the opportunity. One aspect of the selection procedures for new staff was to pay attention to this issue and to design the application and selection process in such a way that these students had an equal opportunity to display their talents. It also meant that once they were selected and participating in the training program, these students needed to have opportunities that allowed them to display their knowledge and skills. The classroom needed to be a safe environment for the usually hesitant student to speak up, share thoughts, and receive feedback. Both group and individual projects needed to be legitimate; and carefully sequenced experiences needed to be provided to enable the X to be more comfortable in doing independent tasks.

Tempering Type Z Professionals. Z type students are highly creative and possess an ability to integrate highly divergent material into a workable whole. They are not afraid of ambiguities and often venture into new and exciting territory. These students can also perform in an erratic manner if their imagination is not captured and their attention not sustained. As graduate students they are aspiring to be professionals in our field and we have the responsibility to aid them in developing the ability to perform in a sustained manner; to help them structure their writing and their verbal communications so that they are understood, and to encourage them to try out their new ideas—but to focus the ideas on pragmatic goals that other professionals will appreciate and understand.

Heath's model also helps us to focus on ourselves as administrators. How do we put people together in task groups, for example? If we assume that the three types in combination cover the skills necessary to complete any project (strengths in organization, innovation, and communication) and the weaknesses to cause a project to fail (hesitancy, obstinacy, inconsistency), we need to select fairly mature individuals from all three types to insure that they could work together to capitalize on their strengths and complete the assignment. But that would involve paying attention to the sub-tasks assignments very carefully so that individual committee members were assigned a task that they found both challenging and rewarding and one that they would enjoy completing. We need to capitalize on the strengths of our staffs (student and professional) and not expect them all to be able to do all things.

Finally, the Heath model may prove to be a useful tool for self assessment. What are the developmental tasks that we find difficult? Where can we seek to enhance our range of skills and abilities? What do we reward or punish in others, and is that a result of *our* style and not necessarily of the performance of others?

references

Agar, J. "The Construction of an Instrument to Assess Heath Typologies in a Resident Advisor Population." Unpublished master's thesis, University of Maryland, 1978.

Erikson, E. *Identity: Youth and Crisis.* New York: W. W. Norton and Co., 1968.

Heath, R. *The Reasonable Adventurer.* Pittsburgh: University of Pittsburgh Press, 1964.

Heath, R. "Form, Flow, and Full-being." *The Counseling Psychologist,* 1973, *4,* 56-63.

Heath, R. "The Key to the Modes of Existence Test." Unpublished mimeograph, 1976a.

Heath, R. "The Modes of Existence Test." Unpublished mimeograph, 1976b.

Hillman, L. "Superimposing Models: William G. Perry, Jr., and Roy Heath." Unpublished manuscript, University of Maryland, 1978.

Loevinger, J. *Ego-Development: Conceptions and Theories.* San Francisco: Jossey-Bass, 1977.

Tyler, L. *Individuality: Human Possibilities and Personal Choice in the Psychological Development of Men and Women.* San Francisco: Jossey-Bass, 1978.

Wertheimer, L. "The Reasonable Adventurer as Relativist." Unpublished manuscript, University of Maryland, 1976.

*Change has always been a part of higher education
and there have always been "new" students catalyzing
a creative tension between their needs and the
traditional ways and means of universities.*

new students:
challenge to
student affairs

adrienne barna
james r. haws
lee knefelkamp

American higher education has a history of being both responsive to the needs of the society it serves and reflective of the changing nature of that society. Even the briefest survey of higher education in this country demonstrates consistent changes in the characteristics of college students and the characteristics of the institutions in which they study. Our recent concern with populations of students "new" to our nation's campuses needs to be seen in the context of the history of higher education in America (Cross, 1976). We may divide the history into three major periods, each representing a different philosophical stance toward the purpose of higher education. The shifts from one stance to another were reflected in changes in the curriculum and student populations.

Colleges in the early, Aristocratic Period, were characterized as private, high tuition institutions which offered only a narrow number of fields of study (law, medicine, theology) and existed primarily to prepare upperclass males to assume their place in the leadership of society. The vast majority of students came from monied families of high social status. They were not necessarily highly motivated or academically able, but their socio-economic position afforded them admission. The poor, ethnic minorities, and women (with the exception of those who attended finishing schools) were excluded; it was assumed that higher education was not needed to prepare them for their positions in society.

There was a major philosophical shift from the philosophy of Aristocracy to one of Meritocracy that began with the Land Grant Period and lasted to the 1950s. The nation now paired educational opportunities with ability, with the earned right to an education. The "new" students of this period came primarily from working and middle class families and had excellent performance records in secondary schools. They demanded an expanded curriculum that reflected their interests and expanded employment goals. There was a marked increase of women and veterans, and a modest increase in minority enrollment. Colleges reflected the philosophy that the society needed to promote and use its intellectual resources regardless of socio-economic status. New public land grant institutions were characterized by lower tuitions and expanded curricula—expanded to meet the needs of the explosion of professional roles and careers available in an industrialized society. The role of higher education underwent a consistent expansion and democratization during the late forties and early fifties. A number of national commissions called for an expanded concept of *who* should benefit from higher education. College and university ranks were swelled by the ever greater percentage of high school graduates entering college and by the large number of WW II and Korean Conflict veterans attending school on the G.I. Bill. However democratic these changes were, barriers persisted that resulted in under-representation of students from minority groups and lower socio-economic classes: (1) the new emphasis on academic performance and national testing systems; (2) the ability to pay (despite increases in financial aid programs); and (3) the societal view of what were appropriate roles for women and minorities.

The period of the sixties and early seventies brought the most radical shift in the nation's concept of higher education. It is called the Period of Egalitarianism and reflects the increasing pressure from broad segments of the population to change the face of higher education. These "new" students (minorities, women, life-long learners, physically handicapped, and academically less able) demanded admission, financial aid, and significant changes in the programs, curricula, and the very structure of the institutions themselves. There was a dramatic increase of ethnic minorities and of minority and majority students with low-academic records and test scores. Frequent references are now made to the "adult learner" and the "returning" woman or man. Federal legislation extended the concept of equal access to include the physically handicapped. More and more students from lower socio-economic backgrounds saw the college degree as having a direct relationship to a better job and the way "up" in the society. Colleges and universities changed too. State schools expanded in size and number (junior and community colleges, branches of state universities). Schools began or expanded remedial and tutorial programs and experimented with open admissions. There were changes in the grading system and even more flexible class schedules to accommodate the new learners, and changes in degree programs and curriculum at both the graduate and undergraduate level.

Change has always been a part of higher education and there have always been "new" students coming to the campuses, catalyzing a creative tension between the needs of these new students and the traditional ways and means of college and university environments. These students' needs have consistently resulted in new programs, alternative delivery systems, and even in new types of institutions being developed. Generations of students have challenged and changed the basic academic assumptions of higher education in the past. However, Cross (1971, 1976) suggests that the "new student" now entering our colleges in large numbers have such different characteristics and needs as learners that their challenge has revolutionary implications. Cross' New Students of the Seventies are distinguished more by their low academic test scores than by any other single measure, including race, sex, and socioeconomic status. They are defined as those students who:

1. have scores in the lowest one third among national samples of high school students taking the traditional academic ability tests,
2. have had consistent difficulty performing traditional academic tasks throughout their academic experience, and
3. do not find present forms of education to be appropriate or adequate.

While a substantial number of the New Students who fit this definition are from minority groups, most are Caucasians whose fathers work at blue-collar jobs. These students are first generation college attenders who most often attend local community colleges or large public institutions. They have generally not been successful in high school, and are less interested than traditional students in the process of learning for learning's sake. They see education as a means to a better life than their parents have experienced.

previous educational experiences

Their previous educational experiences have been characterized by a constant threat of failure; and by an environment that is designed to reward skills and abilities that they do *not* possess and to ignore those areas of skill and ability that they *do* possess. They have all too often become trapped in a self-defeating academic cycle in which high achievers remain at the top while the less achievement oriented are neglected and sink lower and lower. Thus they have been characterized (Atkinson and Feather, 1966; Cross, 1971) as "failure threatened personalities"—those individuals who avoid tasks in which the outcome is uncertain and in which they are required to take risks. Such individuals tend to defend against the threat of failure either by selecting easy tasks where success is assured, or by attempting such difficult tasks that failure is clearly expected and is therefore not threatening to one's sense of self. Cross considers the existence of this pattern to be a partial explanation for the unrealistic academic expectations that they have when entering colleges and universities. These students have often not had the opportunity to develop realistic expectations of themselves or of education. When faced with difficulties in the academic environment they often become passive, cease to put forth effort, and stop trying to succeed. Cross cites this pattern of "lack of effort and quitting the task" as the highest ranked obstacle to learning for low-achieving students. The picture is one of students who will have enormous difficulty meeting the challenges and the requirements of traditional academic institutions and will find little support or appreciation for the skills that they do possess. Clearly, the New Student has life-long experience with the reality that learning is an ego-threatening task. They have been uncomfortable and unrewarded in previous educational environments, and are likely to repeat those experiences in our colleges and universities unless new approaches are found to restructure their learning environments.

personality characteristics

In addition to the difficulties presented by their history, New Students have a number of other characteristics that inhibit them in most university environments: (a) they are much less autonomous than their traditional student peers and much more dependent on authority figures for structure and guidance; (b) they tend to have difficulty with viewpoints and individuals that differ with their own perspectives and thus might be expected to have difficulty with the great diversity of people and ideas that higher education has to offer; (c) they have markedly less self-confidence in their intellectual skills than their peers and are more eager for and expectant of assistance with their academic work—at the same time that they are hesitant to seek it out; (d) their interest patterns show them to lack interest in scholarly pursuits and to be interested in activities that are decidedly non-intellectual in nature. Hence, they are not likely to feel rewarded by the educational environment, nor are they likely to find the environment attending to their areas of interest and concern; (e) they are individuals who have a low tolerance for ambiguity and delayed gratification, and have difficulty adjusting to the essentially vicarious learning tasks of higher education. Perhaps most importantly, New Students tend to prefer those activities "that require low levels of cognitive skills and that also stress physical-social content as opposed to intellectual-aesthetic interests" (Maier and Anderson, 1964). Activities of that kind "impose few specific demands on the participant, do not provide much feedback to use in guiding action, invite passivity, and provide immediate gratification." Such activities are not conducive to growth in cognitive complexity. Maier and Anderson emphasize the lack of cognitive experiences in the environments of the New Student, and they consider this lack as the primary impediment to their development in college. They, like many of the theorists we have reviewed in previous chapters, believe that cognitive abilities can be developed when the student's readiness to learn and the appropriate learning experiences are brought together. Cross also supports this interactionist view of development and calls for college and university faculty and administrators to begin to address the serious task of redesigning and restructuring our present learning environments to be more responsive to the needs of these students. Cross reminds us that the greatest differences between New Students and traditional students is on the cognitive/non-cognitive dimension.

career interests and expectations of higher education

New Students demonstrate very clear patterns of interest, positive motivation, and satisfactions in the area of vocationally oriented curricula. They often come to college with a career choice made and see their higher educational experience in very pragmatic terms. They expect that the college degree will yield tangible rewards like a secure job and greater salary earning potential. Thus, they are not prepared for the reality that traditional higher education curricula are not directly related to vocational concerns. They come to the campuses expecting that the environment will be friendly and vocationally oriented. This is in direct contrast to their more traditional peers who also want a friendly campus, but who are seeking a more academically oriented one. New Students indicate that they want a great deal of student/faculty contact and assistance. They also indicate that they see college as helpful in improving their interpersonal skills abilities.

strengths

New Students bring many strengths to their educational experience, although many of them may not be directly rewarded by the environment. They indicate a willingness to use the advice and service of faculty, advisors, counselors, and administrators. They are eager for help with study skills, reading speed and comprehension, educational-vocational counseling, employment, financial aid, and personal counseling. The difficulty lies with their hesitancy to seek that help on their own, especially their tendency to become passive in the face of adversity. New students generally have more developed mechanical and physical skills than their more traditional peers; and, because they so often work and live off campus, they often have solid "instrumental autonomy" skills. They are motivated to make a better life for themselves, they are able to put forth great effort when they understand the tasks they are asked to do. If provided the proper structure, they can accomplish much by their efforts, but they need help in generating the structure.

implications for student affairs

The work of Patricia Cross stands as a direct challenge to those of us who have embraced a profession philosophically based on the assessment of individual student needs and the design of programs to meet those needs. She brings to us a sociological perspective on students, one that analyzes their abilities and previous experiences and finds that there exists a woeful mismatch between the needs and expectations of a student population and the expectations and services of the traditional educational environment. Her work demands an examination of our educational environments and their pressure on students, and of the means of assessing *both* new and traditional students. She reminds us that we have the responsibility to assess needs and design developmentally conducive environments for all our students, although she would clearly assert that the New Student is the least prepared and therefore the most needy. Hers is a clear and simply stated challenge: Can we have education for all, and also education for each? Can we really individualize mass education? We believe that there are a variety of roles that the student affairs practitioner can play in meeting this challenge.

1. Perhaps the most important is the role of Faculty Consultant. Most faculty have little formal preparation in the skills of teaching and have little understanding of the learner characteristics of their students, especially of the New Student. We have knowledge of college student development and learner characteristics and can work in a consulting role with faculty subject matter experts to design more effective teaching-learning environments that would help maximize the learning for both traditional and New Students. This educational partnership can do much to expand the processes that are used in teaching the important content and concept material. For example, there is much that can be done through the use of cognitive level matching models that would help the instructor both understand his student and deliver the material in ways that would be appropriate for the level of students in the class. Many of these models have been discussed in previous chapters on the work of William Perry and Lawrence Kohlberg. The entire area of educational technology has immense promise for our work with the New Student. There are many concrete, pragmatic, rapid feedback learning aids that would help the New Student learn the content and concepts in ways that capitalized on their strengths and did not emphasize their weaknesses. Scores of colleges and universities have been experimenting with non-traditional learning options that might be appropriate for the New Student. Much of this information is not widely known to the average faculty member. The student personnel worker as faculty consultant could provide much of the educational psychology and technology knowledge that could be used in combination with the knowledge and skills of the faculty to enhance the learning environments on our campuses.

2. Academic Advising and Career Counseling are two additional areas of critical importance. There is a need to expand both services to seek out the New Students and to help them with the structuring and sequencing of their educational experiences. Advisors and counselors would perhaps be more effective if they began their contact with these students while they were still in high schools—helping to explain and prepare them for the higher education world and establishing contact with them early so that they could break their passive cycle and seek help when it was needed. We need to expand our own perspectives of the purposes of higher education and consider the appropriateness of being able to counsel students with respect to non-white collar and professional jobs. Much of the college counseling is tinged with a "professional" bias that does not reflect the aspirations of many of the New Students.

3. Orientation offices can do much to help the New Student adjust to the new environment. Careful attention to their characteris-

tics can be reflected in orientation programs that help the student learn how to manage the environment, that bring to their attention the tasks and expectations of the academic community and how they can find help with those tasks.

4. Our Activities Programs and Unions can provide outlets for the strengths and skills and interests of New Students by attending to their needs in programming. If the students can find activities that involve them and meet their needs, they will likely be able to build on those positive experiences as sources of support.

5. Tutorial and Study Skill programs need to be expanded and made more available to these students. Emphasis needs to be placed on skills and on becoming more cognitively complex so that the students are prepared to understand the tasks they are expected to perform.

6. We need to become accurate assessors of the university environment as a whole and its sub-environments. We need to be able to describe those environments and the pressure they exert on students with great precision. Then we can begin realistic work in helping the student understand the reality of the environment they are entering and how to prepare for it. Many assessment instruments are available and could be used to provide a data bank of environmental information that would be analyzed with respect to its potential impact on the students working within the environments.

7. We have a role of advocate that needs to be played. Administrators and faculty members need to know who the New Students are, what their needs, strengths and weaknesses are, and what programs are necessary to help meet those needs. They are currently an increasing population on our large public campuses, and the campuses are not prepared to understand them, instruct them adequately, or to welcome the diversity and challenge they bring. We can educate and advocate.

8. Lastly, the "new" new student and our need to respond serves as a reminder that college and university population is becoming more diversified every year. We need to be in a posture of flexibility to students' needs and of upholding standards of performance and excellence that represent higher education. But we need to be open to the possibilities of alternative ways of demonstrating skills and competencies, to the fact that cognitive skills cannot be separated from other areas of a student's life, and that higher education has flourished in this country because it has been able to respond to the changing needs and challenges of its citizens.

references

Atkinson, J. W. and Feather, N. T. *A Theory of Achievement Motivation.* New York: John Wiley & Sons, 1966.

Cross, K. P. *Beyond the Open Door: New Students to Higher Education.* San Francisco: Jossey-Bass, 1971.

Cross, K. P. *Accent on Learning: Improving Instruction and Reshaping the Curriculum.* San Francisco: Jossey-Bass, 1976.

Maier, M., and Anderson, S. *Growth Study: Adolescent Behavior and Interests.* Research Bulletin RB-64-52. Princeton, N.J.: Educational Testing Service, 1964.

Adrienne Barnais a doctoral student in the Counseling and Personnel Services Department at the University of Maryland. She is presently on the staff of the Faculty Associate to the Vice Chancellor for Student Affairs at the university.

James R. Haws is a doctoral student in the Counseling and Personnel Services Department at the University of Maryland. He has been on the staff of the Faculty Associate to the Vice Chancellor for Student Affairs and is presently doing an internship at the University of Maryland Counseling Center.

references

The resources for the study of college students are extensive as is indicated by the length of the references to each chapter. We have attempted to select one or two key references from those lists that present the basic structure of thought in the theory. The monograph and these references might form the reading list for an introductory course on college student development or serve as an update for practitioners.

Chickering, A. W. *Education and Identity*. San Francisco: Jossey-Bass, 1969.
> This is one of the few explicit attempts to relate theory to practice. Chickering analyzes the elements of the university which have the potential to encourage student development.

Cross, K. P. *Accent on Learning: Improving Instruction and Reshaping the Curriculum*. San Francisco: Jossey-Bass, 1976.
> Consideration is given to the learning styles and problems of the New Learners. A must for understanding the challenge presented to higher education by this population.

Erikson, E. "Identity and the Life Cycle." *Psychological Issues Monograph*, Vol. I (1). New York: International Universities Press, 1959.
> This is the most complete single discussion of the Identity step. Later works refine the discussion, but this is fundamental.

Heath, D. "A Model of Becoming a Liberally Educated and Mature Student." In C. Parker (Ed.) *Encouraging Development in College Students*. Minneapolis: University of Minnesota Press, 1978.
> Contains the basic rationale for the model with a good description of the self systems and developmental dimensions. Persons looking for research support should see *Maturity and Competence: a Transcultural View*. New York: Gardner Press, 1977.

Heath, R. "Personality and the Development of Students in Higher Education." In C. Parker (Ed.), *Encouraging Development in College Students*. Minneapolis: University of Minnesota Press, 1978.
> This is Heath's most recent description of his model. He relates it to other typologies and provides the basic research support.

Keniston, K. *Youth and Dissent*. New York: Harcourt Brace Jovanovich, Inc., 1971.

    Keniston was one of the most careful observers of youth in the sixties. This is a compilation of published papers written through that decade and held together in this volume by the exposition of the Stage of Youth.

King, P. M. *The Development of Reflective Judgment and Formal Operational Thinking in Adolescents and Young Adults*. Unpublished doctoral dissertation, University of Minnesota, 1977.

    Contains the most complete review of research on the Perry scheme completed to data.

Kohlberg, L. "Stage and Sequence: The Cognitive Developmental Approach to Socialization." In D. Goslin (Ed.), *Handbook of Socialization Theory and Research*. Chicago: Rand McNally, 1969.

    While there are several good introductions to Kohlberg, this is one of the more complete.

Levinson, D., and others. *The Season's of a Man's Life*. New York: Alfred A. Knopf, 1978.

    Adult development has become an important concern in recent years. Levinson presents one usable formulation of total life span development worthy of further consideration.

Loevinger, J. *Ego Development: Conceptions and Theories*. San Francisco: Jossey-Bass, 1976.

    The theory of ego development is defined, described and compared with other theories of personality.

Parker, C. A. *Encouraging the Development of College Students*. Minneapolis: University of Minnesota Press, 1978.

    A discussion of attempts to use developmental theory in both the curriculum and student affairs. Includes program descriptions and reflective comments by developmental theorists.

Parker, C. A. "On Modeling Reality." *Journal of College Student Personnel*, 1977, *18*, 419–425.

    The dilemmas, paradoxes, and problems of using student development theories in practice are illustrated.

Perry, W. G., Jr. *Forms of Intellectual and Ethical Development in the College*, New York: Holt, Rinehart and Winston, 1970.

Contains a complete description of the research design, the scheme as derived from the protocols and good examples of the protocols. Fundamental to understanding the theory.

index

NEW DIRECTIONS QUARTERLY SOURCEBOOKS

New Directions for Student Services is one of several distinct series of quarterly sourcebooks published by Jossey-Bass. The sourcebooks in each series are designed to serve both as *convenient compendiums* of the latest knowledge and practical experience on their topics and as *life-long reference tools.*

One-year, four-sourcebook subscriptions for each series cost $15 for individuals (when paid by personal check) and $25 for institutions, libraries, and agencies. Current 1978 sourcebooks are available by subscription only (however, multiple copies—five or more—are available for workshops or classroom use at $5 per copy).

A complete listing is given below of current sourcebooks in the *New Directions for Student Services* series. The titles and editors-in-chief of the other series are also listed. To subscribe, or to receive further information, write: New Directions Subscriptions, Jossey-Bass Inc., Publishers, 433 California Street, San Francisco, California 94104.

New Directions for Student Services
Ursula Delworth and Gary R. Hanson, Editors-in-Chief
1978 1. Evaluating Program Effectiveness, Gary R. Hanson
2. Training Competent Staff, Ursula Delworth
3. Reducing the Dropout Rate, Lee Noel

New Directions for Community Colleges
Arthur M. Cohen, Editor-in-Chief;
Florence B. Brawer, Associate Editor

New Directions for Child Development
William Damon, Editor-in-Chief

New Directions for Education and Work
Lewis C. Solmon, Editor-in-Chief

New Directions for Experiential Learning
Morris T. Keeton, Editor-in-Chief

New Directions for Higher Education
JB Lon Hefferlin, Editor-in-Chief